W9-BIU-590

THE 100 GREATEST BASEBALL PLAYERS OF ALL TIME

By the same authors

The Image of Their Greatness

By Lawrence Ritter

The Glory of Their Times

By Donald Honig

Baseball When the Grass Was Real
Baseball Between the Lines
The Man in the Dugout
The October Heroes

(Preceding page) *Ty Cobb in 1913 sliding into third baseman Jimmy Austin of the Yankees*

THE 100 GREATEST BASEBALL PLAYERS OF ALL TIME

Lawrence Ritter and Donald Honig

Crown Publishers, Inc.
New York

ACKNOWLEDGMENTS

Most of the photographs in this book are from the library of the National Baseball Hall of Fame and Museum in Cooperstown, New York, and from the Card Memorabilia Associates, Ltd., of Amawalk, New York. We would like to express our special thanks and appreciation to Jack Redding, librarian of the National Baseball Hall of Fame, and Michael P. Aronstein, president of the Card Memorabilia Associates.

The remaining photographs are from the following sources:

Ronald C. Modra, Port Washington, Wisconsin: pages 134, 172, 200, and 246

New York Daily News: pages 60 and 61

Pittsburgh Press: page 10

Louis Requena, Little Ferry, New Jersey: pages 198–199 and 228

Copyright © 1981 by Lawrence Ritter and Donald Honig

All rights reserved. No part of this book may be reproduced or utilized in any form or by any means, electronic or mechanical, including photocopying, recording, or by any information storage and retrieval system, without permission in writing from the publisher.

Inquiries should be addressed to Crown Publishers, Inc., One Park Avenue, New York, New York 10016

Printed in the United States of America

Published simultaneously in Canada by General Publishing Company Limited

Library of Congress Cataloging in Publication Data

Ritter, Lawrence.
The 100 greatest baseball players of all time.

Includes index.
1. Baseball—United States—Records. 2. Baseball players—United States.   I.   Honig, Donald, joint author.
II. Title.
GV877.R57 1981   796.357′0973   80-23046
ISBN: 0-517-543001

Design: Robert Aulicino

10 9 8 7 6 5 4 3 2 1

First Edition

For Catherine Honig
and
Phil, Gayle, Jill, and Brooks

with love

The "100"

Pete Rose   1
Eddie Collins   5
Roy Campanella   7
Bill Terry   9
Roberto Clemente   11
Jim Palmer   15
"Duke" Snider   17
"Kiki" Cuyler   19
Grover Cleveland Alexander   21
Bob Gibson   25
Bill Dickey   27
"Yogi" Berra   29
Bob Feller   31
Mike Schmidt   35
Ernie Lombardi   37
Jimmie Foxx   39
Sam Crawford   43
Tony Oliva   45
George Foster   47
"Lefty" Grove   49
Luke Appling   53
"Chick" Hafey   55
"Smoky" Joe Wood   57
Willie Mays   59
Jimmy Collins   65
Al Simmons   67
Carl Hubbell   69
Christy Mathewson   71
Tom Seaver   75
"Three-Fingered" Brown   77
George Sisler   79
Lou Gehrig   81
Hank Greenberg   87
Jackie Robinson   89

"Goose" Goslin   93
Herb Score   95
Ty Cobb   97
Lou Brock   101
"Pie" Traynor   105
Luis Aparicio   107
"Rube" Waddell   109
Charlie Gehringer   113
Joe Morgan   115
Mel Ott   117
Sandy Koufax   119
"Whitey" Ford   123
Ernie Banks   125
Stan Musial   127
Hal Chase   129
Warren Spahn   133
Fred Lynn   135
"Home Run" Baker   137
"Babe" Ruth   139
Hank Aaron   147
Ed Walsh   149
Addie Joss   151
Pete Reiser   153
"Mickey" Cochrane   157
Dave Parker   159
"Iron Man" McGinnity   163
Rogers Hornsby   165
"Dazzy" Vance   169
Ross Youngs   171
Johnny Bench   173
Ted Williams   175
Joe Medwick   181
Juan Marichal   183
Napoleon Lajoie   185

Joe DiMaggio   187
Steve Carlton   195
Brooks Robinson   197
Jim Rice   201
"Shoeless" Joe Jackson   203
Frank Robinson   207
Tris Speaker   209
Edd Roush   211
Honus Wagner   213
Steve Garvey   217
"Zack" Wheat   219
"Gabby" Hartnett   221
Mickey Mantle   223
"Cy" Young   227
Carl Yastrzemski   229
Paul Waner   231
Ted Lyons   235
Wes Ferrell   237
Johnny Mize   239
Harry Heilmann   241
Walter Johnson   243
George Brett   247
Robin Roberts   249
"Chief" Bender   251
Frankie Frisch   253
Herb Pennock   257
Eddie Plank   259
Joe Sewell   261
Burleigh Grimes   263
"Arky" Vaughan   265
Rod Carew   267
"Dizzy" Dean   269

An alphabetical listing will be found on page 273.

Introduction

No sport has produced a greater wealth of data than baseball, and no fans are more possessive of their game's statistics than baseball fans. Some numbers have a special aura of their own and are hallowed. The number 56 to a baseball fan immediately conjures up Joe DiMaggio's hitting streak; 714 is Babe Ruth's lifetime home runs; .406 belongs to Ted Williams, the game's last .400 hitter; and 4,191 is not a room in a towering hotel but Ty Cobb's lifetime base hits.

Statistics are clean, pure, final, and—as far as baseball is concerned—sometimes quite misleading. Consequently, men with some of the highest batting averages in baseball history have been omitted from the roster of the players we consider to be the game's 100 greatest, as have some pitchers whose records would also seem to demand their inclusion.

Statistics, however, are relative. The man who batted .320 in an era when the norm for excellence was .350 must be said to have fallen short. Conversely, the man who bats .330 when the norm for excellence is signifi- cantly lower must be given consideration as a candidate for all-time greatness.

Some of the omissions are glaring. Although Early Wynn is one of the 7 pitchers to have won 300 or more games in the twentieth century, he is not included, while Herb Score, with a lifetime win total of 55, is. Some of the game's greatest home-run hitters, including Harmon Killebrew, Eddie Mathews, Ralph Kiner, and Willie McCovey, are not included, while Pete Reiser, who had only 1 really outstanding season, is. To rationalize this, the authors cite what they choose to call the "Smoky Joe Wood Syndrome." In 1912 at the age of 22, Joe Wood had won 34 games for the Red Sox but he hurt his arm the next spring and never recaptured his greatness. Since in this book we are discussing ballplaying greatness as exemplified by relative performance, to omit men like Score, Reiser, and Wood, whose meteoric careers were aborted by injuries, would be to deny our premise. We accept the argument that a lot is being taken on faith—namely, that given injury-free careers these men would have maintained high levels of achievement year after year—but faith is well within the province of baseball fans, who return to the ball parks every spring with hope and devotion.

Also, the number 100 is, like all numbers, quite exact and cannot be stretched. Any enumeration of "greatest" ballplayers, be it 10 or 100 or 1,000, must have a cut-off point. The closer that cut-off point approaches, the more difficult the process of selection becomes.

It was decided to consider only those players who played the bulk of their games after 1900. It was at the turn of the century that the American League was organized and the two-league structure established. To start before 1900 would also have meant assessing the records of players who performed under different rules, including a shorter distance from the pitching mound to home plate. Thus, the alert fan will immediately note the absence of such outstanding old-time performers as Ed Delehanty, Wee Willie Keeler, Amos Rusie, and many others, some of whom did indeed play in the early years of the twentieth century but whose best years occurred before 1900.

There are other omissions, and these are not due to the boundary of time. They are, rather, due to decades of unforgiveable bigotry, when organized baseball was barred to certain American citizens for the reason that their skins were of a darker hue. There is no doubt that a book purporting to represent the greatest ballplayers of all time should include Satchel Paige, Josh Gibson, Cool Papa Bell, John Henry Lloyd, Buck Leonard, Oscar Charleston, and many other old-time Blacks. In their cases, we are unable to document what we know to be true.

Taking an 80-year perspective on a game that has seen thousands and thousands of players come and go turned out to be a more difficult task than was originally anticipated. We were quite frankly dismayed at some of the fine players we were compelled to omit. Some people may question the selection of certain active players, and here again judgments may be legitimately debated. No one can be sure that a few of these players are not going to play themselves right off the list in a few years (some of them are, at this writing, at midpoint in their careers), just as some others not selected may begin to play themselves onto it.

So we must take refuge in the last defense of any compiler of any list of the "greatest": we were conscientious, diligent, objective, and, in the sense that the word applies, as scholarly as we could be, fully aware that next to a close pennant race the thing that excites baseball fans most is a debate about who are the game's greatest players.

THE 100 GREATEST BASEBALL PLAYERS OF ALL TIME

Pete Rose in 1963

Pete Rose

Voted at the end of 1979 by fans and sports writers as the outstanding player of the decade, Pete Rose was an ironic symbol for the 1970s. On the one hand, the way Pete campaigned for a lucrative contract after declaring his free agency in the autumn of 1978 was in the best (or worst) traditions of '70s hucksterism. He flew from city to city showing prospective employers a half-hour documentary film which depicted the feats and adventures of Pete Rose on the baseball diamond.

And that is where the irony comes in—Pete Rose on a baseball diamond. Businessman of the '70s though he is, Rose is a ballplaying throwback to the spirit, hustle, and élan of an earlier time. And it is this sheer, unbridled joy that he takes in playing that has made Rose an all-time favorite of the fans, one of the greatest players in history, a rich man, a happy man, and a legend.

This legend, by his own admission, is not a "natural." He does not possess the blinding running speed of a Mickey Mantle, the fluid swing of a Ted Williams, the instinctive defensive grace of a Joe DiMaggio. Rose has done it by constant practice and brute energy, melding his solid talents with a Cobb-like determination—although playing not with Ty Cobb's grim hatred but with his own blend of joy and belligerence.

Rose came to the big leagues with Cincinnati in 1963 as a second baseman. He subsequently became a left fielder for his hometown team, then a right fielder, then a third baseman, and finally, for the Philadelphia Phillies, a first baseman. An all-star performer at each position, he has led National League outfielders in fielding average 3 times, third basemen once.

But it is what Rose does offensively that has captured the imagination of baseball fans. In his second year in the minor leagues he hit the astounding total of 30 triples, an all-time minor-league record. In his first 2 big-league seasons, 1963 and 1964, he hit .273 and .269. From then on, however, it was to be .300 or better for 14 of the next 15 seasons, picking up 3 batting titles along the way: in 1968, 1969, and 1973. He has established a major-league record for collecting 200 or more hits the most times (10), leading in hits 6 times and in doubles 4 times.

In the summer of 1978, Rose began drawing the attention of fans all around the country as he embarked on a well-publicized hitting streak. A consecutive-game hitting streak is perhaps the most dramatic example of the Rose phenomenon, since it embodies two of his most prominent characteristics: consistency and durability.

Thriving on the drama and the pressure, Rose rode his hitting streak through 44 games before he was stopped, tying the National League record and becoming the first man ever to come within hailing distance of Joe DiMaggio's hitherto unapproachable 56-game record.

In the era of the long ball, Pete Rose has become a titan by hitting singles and doubles.

Pete Rose scoring, Pete Rose style. The date is July 31, 1972. The catcher is the Giants' Dave Rader.

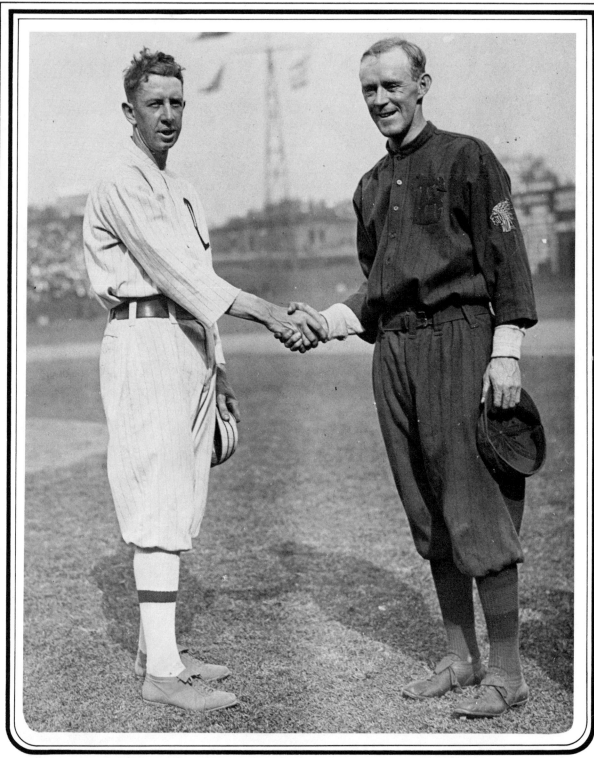

Rival second basemen Eddie Collins (left) and Johnny Evers shaking hands before the opening of the 1914 World Series between the Philadelphia Athletics and Boston Braves

Eddie Collins

Eddie Collins was by all accounts one of the most intelligent men ever to play baseball. Adding this fine intelligence to his abundant natural gifts turned Collins into one of the finest players in the game's history. Indeed, for many years he was the automatic choice for the game's greatest all-time second baseman, in spite of Rogers Hornsby's mammoth batting averages. Those who saw him remembered Collins's brilliant defensive play, his aggressive base running, his many intangibles. It was not until Eddie's grinding day-by-day brilliance began to fade from living memory that Hornsby assumed his place at second base on the all-time team.

When he retired in 1930 after a 25-year career, Collins was second to Ty Cobb in stolen bases, with 743. Eddie's lifetime batting average is .333; he hit over .360 3 times, with a high of .369 in 1920. That was the year the Chicago White Sox should have taken a second consecutive pennant, but it was also the year that the scandal of the 1919 World Series broke and many of the White Sox stars were suspended in September, enabling Cleveland to win a close pennant race. One of the few White Sox regulars to emerge untainted by the scandal was Collins, whom the gamblers knew better than to approach.

Eddie came to the major leagues as a 19-year-old shortstop with Connie Mack's Ath-letics in 1906; 2 years later he took over at second base and remained a regular at the position with the A's and the White Sox until 1926.

A member of the 3,000-hit club, Collins played in 6 World Series and has a Series average of .328 for 34 games.

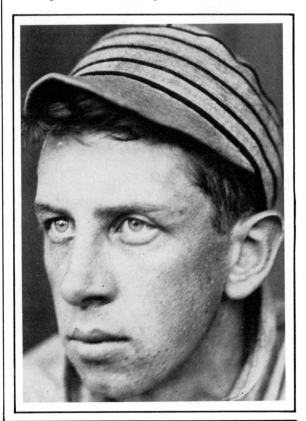

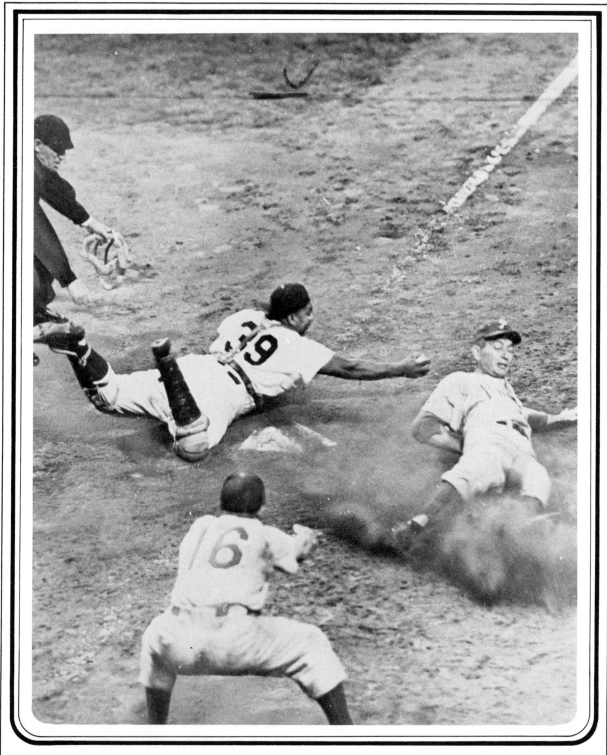

Roy Campanella has just tagged out the Phillies' Eddie Waitkus at Ebbets Field. Number 16 is Mel Clark of the Phillies. The umpire about to go up with the thumb is Larry Goetz.

Roy Campanella

When Roy Campanella showed up in the Brooklyn Dodgers' spring camp in 1948, Dodgers' boss Branch Rickey pronounced him the greatest catcher in baseball. In his next breath Rickey told Roy he was being sent to the Dodgers' St. Paul farm club in the American Association. "Why?" the puzzled Campy said. "Because," Rickey said, "if anybody sees you play ball you'll have to stay with this club. I want you to break the color barrier in the American Association." Muttering that he was a ballplayer and not a pioneer, the best catcher in baseball went to St. Paul.

By midseason Roy was back with the Dodgers and there he remained for 10 years, a power hitter, a flawless defensive catcher, a shrewd handler of pitchers. Playing on what was virtually an all-star team, Roy was a standout, being voted the National League's Most Valuable Player in 1951, 1953, and 1955. Catching 144 games in 1953, Roy batted .312, hit 41 home runs, and drove in a league-leading 142 runs. Those home runs and runs batted in stand as single-season major-league records for a catcher.

On the night of January 28, 1958, as he was driving to his Long Island home, Campanella's car skidded and turned over while he was trying to negotiate an icy curve. He suffered a broken neck and severe damage to his spinal cord. Paralyzed from the neck down, Roy Campanella was destined to spend the rest of his life in a wheelchair.

Roy Campanella in 1949

Bill Terry in 1924

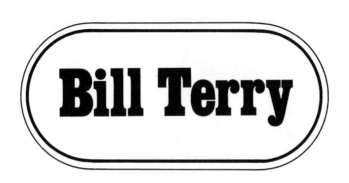

Bill Terry

In the spring of 1922 John J. McGraw's Giants were in Memphis to play an exhibition game. Having heard about a fine young semi-pro player in town, McGraw arranged a meeting with the young man.

"How would you like to play for the Giants?" McGraw asked.

"For how much?" asked young Bill Terry.

McGraw was taken aback. The Giants were at the time the lords of the baseball world, the team on which young ballplayers dreamed of playing. Bill Terry, however, was a tough-minded and independent young man, and neither the New York Giants nor John McGraw impressed him.

He eventually joined the Giants, of course, and became one of the greatest players McGraw ever had, and undoubtedly the greatest first baseman in National League history.

Terry was the complete player. Along with his fine fielding and swiftness afoot went a particularly lethal bat. Among twentieth-century National Leaguers, only Rogers Hornsby's lifetime .358 average tops Terry's .341. In 1930 Bill became the last National Leaguer to hit .400, batting .401 and tying Lefty O'Doul's league record with 254 hits. He got more than 200 hits 6 times, and for 6 consecutive years (1927–1932) he batted in more than 100 runs.

McGraw never did learn to like the blunt-spoken Terry, and the feeling was intensely mutual. In fact, for several years John J. and his great first baseman barely spoke to one another. But when McGraw retired in 1932 with the privilege of choosing his successor, he forgot personalities. Terry was the man he selected. Bill proved the old man right by winning 3 pennants in the next 6 years.

Roberto Clemente acknowledging the applause of the fans after his three thousandth hit

Roberto Clemente

In the star-studded Pittsburgh Pirate lineup, Roberto Clemente was known as "The Great One." The appellation was appropriate. Clemente was one of the most superbly gifted ballplayers ever to appear on the diamond. A wicked line-drive hitter with blazing running speed, he was an incomparable outfielder with a powerful and deadly accurate throwing arm.

Signed by the Brooklyn Dodgers for a $10,000 bonus, Clemente was left unprotected in the 1954 draft and was grabbed by the Pirates on the recommendation of scout Clyde Sukeforth for $4,000—certainly the greatest draft bargain in history. He entered the Pirate outfield in 1955 and remained for 18 seasons. He batted over .300 13 times, with a high of .357 in 1967. He led the league in batting 4 times, twice in hits. In 1966 he was voted the National League's Most Valuable Player.

He was a moody man, filled with a brooding pride. Highly sensitive, he felt he was not adequately recognized, letting it be known that he resented the acclaim that went to such players as Willie Mays, Mickey Mantle, and Frank Robinson. Bobby Bragan, who managed the Pirates when Clemente was a youngster, described him as "a real introvert . . . very quiet, morose almost." Even in those early years Clemente complained of a bad back, an ailment that would plague him throughout his career. Bragan learned not to push his moody young star. "When he didn't want to play, he wouldn't play, and that's all there was to it." But most of the time he did play, and when he did it was with a smoldering fury, going out on the field each day to prove once again with his bat, arm, and legs that he was the best. The men on the field with him always knew how good he was; it took the rest of the country a little time to catch up.

The country caught up in the 1971 World Series. Pittsburgh played a Baltimore club that featured the pitching of 4 20-game winners and that many people considered practically invincible. Going out on that vast stage which is the World Series, Clemente put on a sustained 7-game performance that has few parallels in Series annals. Hitting safely in every game (which he had also done in Pittsburgh's 7-game Series against the Yankees in 1960), Roberto collected 12 hits, including 2 doubles, a triple, and 2 home runs, for a batting average of .414. He covered the outfield as smoothly as the grass and kept base runners honest with several mighty throws. The Pirates won the championship and Roberto Clemente emerged as a bona fide superstar for fans everywhere.

He kept getting better. Beginning in 1969, then 35 years old, he reeled off batting averages of .345, .352, and .341. In 1972, hampered by injuries, he "slumped" to .312. In the final game of the 1972 season he drove out his three thousandth hit, becoming only the eleventh player in major league history to compile so many hits.

Clemente returned to his native Puerto Rico (where he had long been a national hero) after the 1972 season, an 18-year major-league veteran with a lifetime .317 batting average.

Late in December, an earthquake devastated Managua, Nicaragua's capital. Clemente, a deeply feeling man, helped organize a committee to fly food, medicine, and other supplies to the suffering city. On New Year's Eve, Roberto Clemente and several other men took off from San Juan in a small DC-7 of dubious quality. Shortly after takeoff the plane crashed into the ocean. Clemente's body was never found. He can, however, be found deep in the hearts of his countrymen, and in the hearts of baseball fans everywhere; and he can be found in the memories, the legends, and the record books that are part of the game he played so passionately and so well.

Jim Palmer

There are two distinct stages in the distinguished pitching career of Jim Palmer. The first goes back to the middle 1960s, when the 20-year-old right-hander joined the Baltimore Orioles, became a starter, won 15 games in 1966, and topped off his season with a 6–0 blanking of the Los Angeles Dodgers in the World Series. The future seemed limitless for the stylish youngster with the sizzling, rising fastball. The next year he developed arm trouble. He spent the greater part of the 1967 and 1968 seasons in the minor leagues. He was exposed to the baseball draft, but no team was willing to gamble on him. In 1969, however, he recovered from his miseries and made a startling comeback with a 16–4 record, including a no-hitter.

Palmer has never been entirely free from aches and pains since his comeback, but he has pitched often enough and well enough to rack up 20 or more wins 8 times, win 3 Cy Young Awards (1973, 1975, 1976), and post the lowest career earned-run average (2.74) of any American League pitcher in the lively ball era (since 1920).

Through the years Palmer has maintained a sometimes comical love-hate relationship with his manager, Earl Weaver. They bicker on the mound and shout in the clubhouse. But never questioned is Weaver's awesome regard for his ace's talent.

"He's a Hall of Fame pitcher," says Earl.

Of that there is no doubt.

"Duke" Snider

There was a time, in the mid-1950s, when New York baseball fans debated the relative merits of the Yankees' Mickey Mantle, the Giants' Willie Mays, and the Dodgers' Edwin Donald "Duke" Snider. In truth, there was not too much difference among the 3 center fielders, although the later reputations of Mantle and Mays have assumed grander proportions than Snider's.

Snider was not merely a great defensive center fielder, but also a graceful one, in the DiMaggio tradition. Confined by the neighborly walls of Brooklyn's Ebbets Field, the Duke often had to wait until the Dodgers were on the road to show off his tremendous range in the field. But those same cozy walls proved to be juicy targets for his home-run shots. From 1953 through 1957 Snider con-

nected for 40 or more home runs, a National League record he shares with Ralph Kiner. In 1953 he batted .336, in 1954, .341. In 1955 he led the league with 136 runs batted in, in 1956 with 43 home runs.

Snider was one of the most powerful hitters in World Series history. In 6 Series with the Dodgers he hit 11 home runs. Twice, in 1952 and again in 1955, he hit 4 home runs in a Series.

Snider might well have gone on to set other records had the Dodgers not moved to Los Angeles in 1958 and into a freakish ball park with such bizarre dimensions it was almost impossible for a left-handed hitter to drive one out of the park. Nevertheless, Snider ended his career with 407 home runs.

Kiki Cuyler in 1935

"Kiki" Cuyler

When Hazen Shirley "Kiki" Cuyler was in his second season in the Pittsburgh outfield in 1925, Pirate fans began calling him the new Ty Cobb. Well, Kiki was not quite that good, but the comparison gives some idea of his abilities and the excitement he generated on a ball field. Cuyler played the outfield with a quality of derring-do that the fans loved; he could snare a fly ball as well as anyone and fire sizzling line-drive strikes to any base.

In his first full seasons, 1924 and 1925, Cuyler batted .354 and .357. In 1925 he hit 26 triples, a figure exceeded in this century only by another Pirate, Chief Wilson, who hit 36 in 1912. In that season Cuyler also hit 17 home runs, 43 doubles, and overall had 220 hits. In the World Series that year, his base-clearing double against Walter Johnson in the eighth inning of the seventh game drove in the runs that gave Pittsburgh the championship.

Midway in the 1927 season Cuyler had a dispute with manager Donie Bush about where Kiki should hit in the batting order. As a result, the stubborn Bush sat down his hard-hitting outfielder for the remainder of the season. The Pirates won the pennant anyway, and the next season Cuyler was traded to the Cubs.

In 1929 and 1930 he batted .360 and .355 for the Cubs, getting 228 hits in the latter season, in addition to leading the league in stolen bases each year.

Cuyler retired in 1938 with a .321 lifetime batting average.

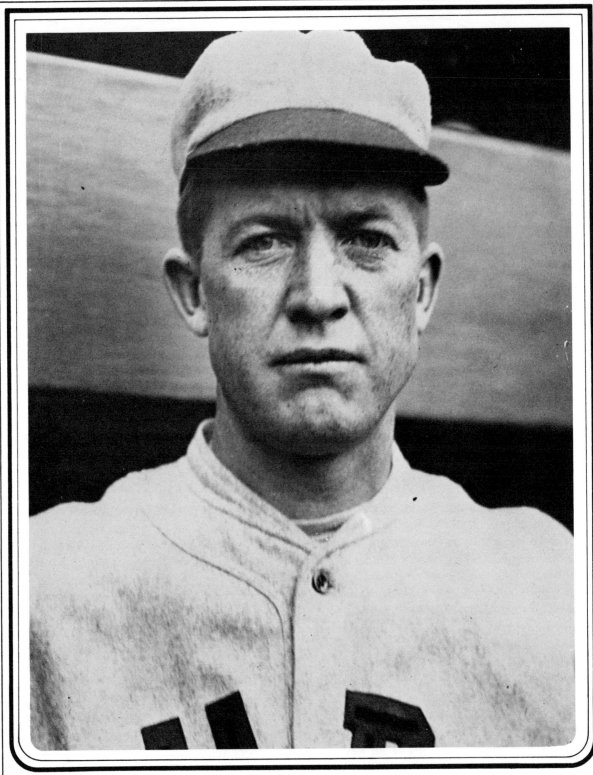

Grover Cleveland Alexander in 1919

Grover Cleveland Alexander

The years of Grover Cleveland Alexander were filled with as much glitter and glory, heartache and tragedy, as there is to be found in the history of American sports.

Alexander's record speaks for itself. The Nebraska farmboy's 373 lifetime victories tie him with Christy Mathewson for the all-time lead among National League pitchers. For 3 consecutive seasons (1915–1917) he was a 30-game winner. For 6 consecutive seasons his earned-run average was never higher than 1.91. In 1916 he pitched a record 16 shutouts, working in a home ball park, Philadelphia's Baker Bowl, that was known as a hitter's paradise and a pitcher's nightmare. His control was uncanny: in 1923 he worked 305 innings and walked but 30 batters. He led the league in shutouts 7 times, wins 6 times, strikeouts 6 times, and earned-run average 5 times.

Alexander, known as Pete to his teammates, averaged better than 27 victories a year his first 7 years in the big leagues. After the 1917 season the Phillies, suspecting their ace would be drafted into the armed forces, sold him to the Cubs. Early in the 1918 season, he was indeed drafted and shipped to France. Sent into action, Alexander endured heavy shelling, that caused a loss of hearing in one ear. And it was in France that he first showed signs of the epilepsy that would plague him for the rest of his life.

When he returned home after the war the lanky, freckled-faced, good-natured pitcher began drinking heavily. He was a changed man; always quiet, he was now introverted. Still effective on the mound—he won 27 for the Cubs in 1920, 22 in 1923—he was no longer the incomparable magician of earlier years.

Whatever demons of war or peace Alexander was trying to exorcise with whiskey refused to depart. He became an alcoholic, sipping his way through the speakeasies of Prohibition America. In 1926, freshman Cub manager Joe McCarthy lost patience with the 39-year-old Alexander and traded him to the Cardinals early in the season.

Alexander pitched creditably for the Cardinals, helping them to their first National

League pennant, which set the stage for his most famous moment. The Cardinals met the mighty Yankees in the World Series that year. Alex pitched complete game victories in the second and sixth games, limiting the Ruth-Gehrig Yankee combine to just 12 hits.

In the seventh game the ghost of past glory appeared once more. Summoned to the mound in the last of the seventh, Alexander was called upon to face the Yankees' rookie slugger Tony Lazzeri with 2 men out and the bases loaded. The Cardinals were ahead by a 3-2 score. It was a classic confrontation, the wizard of the past facing a young dynamo of the future. With his once great speed long gone, Alexander struck out Lazzeri with several sharp, perfectly placed curves to record baseball's most famous strikeout. He shut out the Yankees the next 2 innings to preserve the win and give the Cardinals the World Championship.

He left the big leagues in 1930, weary, ill, drinking heavily. He barnstormed with semi-pro teams for several years. In the early 1940s he was a sideshow attraction in a tawdry Times Square flea circus, describing the Lazzeri strikeout over and over again.

He returned to his native Nebraska in the fall of 1950, frail, sickly, and alone. He took a furnished room in St. Paul, a few miles from the farm in Elba where he had been born. There, on November 4, he died, passing away into the cold, quiet Nebraska night, light-years gone from the cheers and the glory.

Grover Cleveland Alexander in 1914

Grover Cleveland Alexander in spring training with the Cardinals in St. Petersburg, Florida, March 1929

Bob Gibson

One of the hardest-throwing right-handed pitchers in National League history, Bob Gibson was the man who broke Grover Cleveland Alexander's league record for lowest earned-run average in a season. Gibson, who spent all of his 17 big-league seasons in a St. Louis Cardinal's uniform, had his finest year in 1968, when he posted a 1.12 ERA, achieved largely on the strength of a league-leading 13 shutouts. He fanned 268 batters in 304 innings, allowing only 198 hits and 62 walks. Perhaps his most remarkable statistic that year, however, was that with his 22 victories went 9 losses. How Gibson managed to lose 9 games with a 1.12 earned-run average is perhaps best left to the Cardinals' hitters to explain.

Gibson won 20 or better 5 times, with a high of 23 in 1970. A strikeout artist par excellence, his 3,117 strikeouts are a league record. He fanned 200 or more 9 times. His lifetime won-lost record is 251–174.

It is as a World Series performer, however, that Gibson will probably be longest remembered. In the 1964, 1967, and 1968 Series he set a record by winning 7 consecutive games, winning 3 complete games against the Red Sox in the 1967 Series. In the 1968 Series against the Tigers he struck out a record 17 while shutting out Detroit 4–0 in a match-up with 30-game winner Denny McLain. Overall in World Series competition he was 7–2, completed 8 of 9 starts, and struck out 92 in 81 innings.

Bill Dickey

"Bill Dickey made catching look easy," said Charlie Gehringer (who made playing second base look easy). Until Johnny Bench came along to muddy the waters, the choice for the greatest all-time catcher lay between Dickey and his fiery contemporary, Mickey Cochrane.

Dickey's credentials are impressive. His .362 batting average in 1936 remains the highest ever for a catcher. Over his full career he bettered .300 11 times, with a lifetime mark of .313. He also holds the American League record for going through a full season (1931, 125 games) without a passed ball.

Playing on the same team with Babe Ruth and Lou Gehrig (his roommate and close friend) and later with Gehrig and Joe Di-Maggio, Dickey's hitting was often over-shadowed. In 1937 he hit 29 home runs, batted .332, and drove in 133 runs. For 4 consecutive seasons (1936–1939) he drove in more than 100 runs per season. He was the man behind the plate on 8 Yankee pennant winners. His 2-run home run in the fifth game of the 1943 World Series gave the Yankees a 2–0 win over the Cardinals and another World Championship.

At the age of 36 Dickey joined the navy, after the 1943 season. In May of 1946 Joe McCarthy resigned as Yankee manager and Bill Dickey took over. The great catcher was not comfortable managing, however, and left the job before the season was over.

Yogi Berra in the Yankee dugout on April 17, 1964, his first game as Yankee manager

"Yogi" Berra

With Lawrence Peter "Yogi" Berra arriving the year Bill Dickey retired, the Yankees were able to receive uninterrupted Hall of Fame service behind the plate for 35 years. A most unlikely looking athlete, the likable Berra was blessed with one of the game's most graceful swings and with an almost priceless nickname.

Berra starred for a dynasty that was at its most potent during his 18-year career in New York. In the 17 full seasons that he was with them, the Yankees won 14 pennants. As the years went on, Yogi became appreciated more and more. There never was any question about his hitting. Often swinging at pitches far out of the strike zone, golfing line drives over the first baseman's head, he had 10 straight years with 20 or more home runs and 5 times knocked in over 100 runs in a season. A power hitter with a keen eye, he struck out just 12 times in 597 at bats in 1950. He was particularly dangerous in the late innings with men on base.

Berra also became, to the surprise of some who were put off by his malapropisms and his initial awkwardness, one of the shrewdest handlers of pitchers and most deft defensive catchers in the game, once handling 950 chances over 148 straight games without an error—both major-league records for catchers.

Yogi was voted the league's Most Valuable Player 3 times, in 1951, 1954, and 1955. In 1964 he was a surprise choice to succeed Ralph Houk as manager of the Yankees. Despite winning the pennant, he was released after the World Series. Later he returned as a coach, but not before managing the Mets for several years and winning another pennant with them in 1973.

Bob Feller in 1938

Bob Feller

Bob Feller remains baseball's only prodigy. At the age of 17 he made headlines, at the age of 18 he was a regular big-league starter, at the age of 19 he was breaking records. Before he turned 23 he had already recorded seasons of 24–9, 27–11, and 25–13. He was on his way toward establishing what probably would have been unbreakable records when his career was interrupted by military service. He spent the better part of 4 seasons in the United States Navy.

He was born in Van Meter, Iowa. Tutored by a baseball-loving father when they could spare the time from working their farm, the powerful, high-kicking youngster became a local phenomenon—such a phenomenon that he went straight from pitching on the sandlots of Iowa to facing intimidating big-league hitters.

His discovery by Cleveland scout Cy Slapnicka in 1935 is as much a storybook tale as the rest of Feller's career. Badgered for almost a year by some local umpires to come out and see the boy, Slapnicka finally stopped off in Van Meter on his way out west on a

scouting trip, more to appease the umpires than anything else. When he saw the farmboy pitch, however, Slapnicka's eyes almost bulged out of his head. He never did make his trip out west—he stayed put until he had Feller's signature on a contract. As a bonus Bob received a dollar bill and a baseball. Slapnicka returned to Cleveland to tell his employers he had just signed "the greatest pitcher in history." He may have been right.

Was Feller faster than Walter Johnson? The difference between them was so slight as to be irrelevant. It is unlikely that Johnson ever threw harder than Feller did in an exhibition game against the St. Louis Cardinals—the famous Gashouse Gang—in July 1936. The unknown 17-year-old youngster, traveling with the Cleveland Indians but still not on the roster, struck out 8 in 3 innings. The rocket had been launched at full blast. Feller was added to the roster.

Later that season he set an American League record when he struck out 17 Philadelphia Athletics. On the last day of the 1938 season the 19-year-old Feller established a

Cleveland Indians' player-manager Lou Boudreau (left) *and his ace pitcher, Bob Feller*

new major league record for strikeouts in a single game when he fanned 18 batters on a hard-hitting Detroit Tiger club.

Throwing an almost unhittable curve along with his searing fastball, Feller was getting better and better as the war approached. He led the American league 3 straight years in wins, strikeouts, and shutouts. Among his achievements was the only opening-day no-hitter ever pitched, against the White Sox on April 16, 1940.

When baseball resumed its normal look in 1946, some people wondered whether his years away from the game might have taken the edge off Feller's fastball. The answer came early in the season. On April 30 Rapid Robert no-hit the powerful New York Yankees, winning 1–0 on a ninth-inning home run by his catcher Frank Hayes. Feller was brilliant that afternoon, striking out 11 Yankees in a lineup that included Phil Rizzuto, Charley Keller, Tommy Henrich, Joe DiMaggio, Joe Gordon, and Bill Dickey.

It was a prophetic performance, for 1946 was to be Feller's greatest season. He set a new major-league strikeout record with 348, won 26 games, completed 36 of 42 starts, and had 10 shutouts.

Feller was to pitch another no-hitter in 1951, and in addition pitched 12 1-hitters, a record.

After waiting for 12 years, Feller finally got

Bob Feller in 1937

into a World Series in 1948, against the Braves. He pitched a brilliant opening game for Cleveland, but lost a 2-hitter to Johnny Sain, 1–0, on an eighth-inning single by Tommy Holmes which followed a disputed pickoff play at second base. Feller had apparently picked off base runner Phil Masi, but umpire Bill Stewart called him safe. Films later showed that Stewart may have made a bad call.

Like Ted Williams, Joe DiMaggio, Hank Greenberg, and others, Feller lost prime years because of military service. What his awesome statistics would look like if those 4 seasons could be added to his record is something baseball fans, those incorrigible romantics, like to contemplate. Add at least 100 victories to his 266, and at least another 1,000 strikeouts to his 2,581 (which would make him the all-time leader, ahead of Walter Johnson). But as the blunt, unsentimental Feller himself said when the intriguing question was put to him, "We'll never know, will we?"

Mike Schmidt

For years and years fans making up their all-time all-star team had an automatic choice for third base—Pie Traynor, given his credentials at bat and in the field. In a few years, however, there may be some room for debate, assuming Mike Schmidt continues performing as he has been.

Schmidt's slugging has been impressive and consistent. In 1974–1976 he led the National League in home runs, with totals of 36, 38, and 38. In 1977 he hit another 38, in 1979 45, and in 1980 a league-leading 48. In 5 seasons he has driven in over 100 runs, leading the National League with 121 in 1980. He also starred in the 1980 World Series, with 2 home runs, 7 runs batted in, and a .381 batting average.

On April 17, 1976, the Philadelphia third baseman put on one of the greatest 1-game slugging exhibitions in history. In a 10-inning game against the Cubs, he hit 4 home runs in 4 consecutive plate appearances (tying a record) and had 17 total bases, a new record for extra-inning games. By hitting home runs in his next 2 games he tied records for homers in 2 and 3 consecutive games.

Although Schmidt's power hitting may or may not ultimately equal that of another third baseman, Eddie Mathews, it is Mike's remarkable fielding along with his hitting that elevates him to a place among the game's greatest players. His quickness, his range afield, and his throwing arm make him one of the finest defensive third basemen ever. In 1974 he established a league record for third basemen with 404 assists.

The National League's premier catchers in the 1930s, Ernie Lombardi (left) and *Gabby Hartnett, before the 1936 All-Star game*

Ernie Lombardi

Big, powerful, likable catcher Ernie Lombardi played 17 years in the big leagues, from 1931 through 1947, and left behind 2 solid legends. One was that he was probably the slowest runner of all time; the other was that he could hit a baseball as hard as any man who ever lived. A pronounced pull hitter, the right-handed Lombardi sent shortstops and third basemen back to the outfield grass when he came to bat. For the infielders it was both good tactics and good sense—no one wanted to be too close to Ernie's bulletlike line drives. As a consequence, he was deprived of many base hits, being thrown out at first base from short left field.

Nevertheless, enough of Lombardi's rockets landed safely to give him a lifetime batting average of .306 and individual seasons of .343 (1935), .333 (1936), .334 (1937), a league-leading .342 (1938), and another batting title in 1942 with .330. (Another Cincinnati catcher, Bubbles Hargrave, is the only other backstop to lead either league in batting, doing it in 1926.) Ernie hit over .300 10 times and, as further evidence to his prowess at the plate, only once in his career did he strike out as many as 25 times in a single season.

A man of great strength, 6 feet 3 inches tall, weighing a solid 230 pounds, Lombardi on many occasions would reach out with his bare right hand to gather in a wide pitch rather than shift to get it. A good receiver with a strong arm, Ernie played the bulk of his career with Cincinnati and was the man behind the plate in both of Johnny Vander Meer's consecutive no-hitters in 1938.

Jimmie Foxx

It used to be something of a ritual in American League ball parks. A rookie would be nudged in the ribs by a veteran who would point to some impossibly distant spot beyond the fence and say, "That's where Foxx hit it."

How far did Jimmie's incredible home run off Lefty Gomez in Yankee Stadium travel? "I don't know how far it went," Gomez said, "but I do know it takes forty-five minutes to walk up there."

What about the one he hit in the 1930 World Series against the Cardinals? "We were watching it for two innings," said bullpen pitcher Jim Lindsey after the game.

They called him the right-handed Babe Ruth. They talked about his monumental long-distance hitting, his great physical strength (he was known as "The Beast"), and his amiable good nature. He was one of the most genuinely liked men ever to play big-league ball.

He was the personification of the home-run hitter, and appropriately enough was sent to Connie Mack in 1925 by his minor-league manager and fellow Marylander, Frank

"Home Run" Baker, who had starred for Mack's Athletics a decade before. The 17-year-old Foxx, then a catcher, got into a few games and went 6 for 9 in pinch-hitting roles. Jimmie knew what he was doing right from the beginning.

Mack played him at third base for a while, then shifted him to first base in 1929 and there "Double X" remained the bulk of the time through a career that lasted until 1945.

When Foxx retired in 1945 at the age of 38, his 534 lifetime home runs were second only to Babe Ruth's 714. (Today Jimmie is seventh on the all-time list.) Foxx led the American League 4 times in home runs, with a high of 58 in 1932. This may not seem like a great many home-run titles for a man of Foxx's power, but remember that Jimmie was playing in the same league as Babe Ruth, Lou Gehrig, Hank Greenberg, and Joe DiMaggio; winning power-hitting titles in that company was not easy. As a case in point, in 1938 Foxx hit 50 home runs for the Red Sox and wasn't even close to the top—Hank Greenberg put away 58 that year.

Jimmie Foxx in 1939

Foxx's record as an RBI man is probably even more impressive than his home-run hitting. He shares with Babe Ruth and Lou Gehrig the record for most years batting in 100 or more runs—13. Foxx and Gehrig did it in consecutive years, a record they jointly hold. Jimmie led the league 3 times in runs batted in, with such sumptuous totals as 169 in 1932, 163 in 1933, and 175 in 1938.

Foxx hit for average, too, with a lifetime mark of .325. In 1933 his .356 batting average and in 1938 his .349 were good enough to lead the league. In 1933 he won the Triple Crown. In 3 World Series with the Athletics (1929–1931), Jimmie batted .344. In 1932, 1933, and 1938 he was the American League's Most Valuable Player, beating out competition like Babe Ruth, Lou Gehrig, Hank Greenberg, Charlie Gehringer, and Joe DiMaggio, to mention only a few.

Foxx was the big cannon on the great Philadelphia Athletic teams of the late 1920s and early 1930s, along with Mickey Cochrane and Al Simmons. A combination of Connie Mack's tight grip on a dollar and the Depression kept Foxx out of the big money. In 1935 Mack sold him to the Red Sox, where a generous Tom Yawkey paid him well, but soon Jimmie was moving into the down side of his career.

Liked and admired by everyone who knew him, Foxx had but one enemy—himself. A prodigious drinker in his later years, Jimmie ran into nothing but hard luck after leaving baseball. What little money he had taken out of the game he lost in a series of ill-judged investments. And the drinking never stopped.

In July of 1967, a few months short of his sixtieth birthday, Jimmie Foxx choked to death on a piece of meat while dining with his brother in Miami. It was a sad and depressing ending for the friendly man who had come to the big leagues at the age of 17 and gone on to carve out one of the game's most illustrious careers.

Jimmie Foxx and Connie Mack

Sam Crawford in 1908

Sam Crawford

Sam Crawford, the greatest ballplayer ever to come out of Wahoo, Nebraska, was one of the hardest hitters of his time. There are some people who feel that had Sam played in the lively ball era he might have challenged Babe Ruth's supremacy. Playing from 1899 through 1917, mostly in the Detroit Tigers outfield, Sam did the next best thing to hitting home runs—he hit triples. And he hit them with greater frequency than any man in baseball history.

The left-handed-hitting Crawford's mastery of the 3-base hit is remarkable. His 312 3-baggers is the all-time record; Ty Cobb is second with 297. Honus Wagner and Tris Speaker are the only other players to get over 200 triples in the modern era. Crawford is tied with "Shoeless" Joe Jackson for the American League record for 3-base hits in a season (26 in 1914). He led the American League in his favorite hit 5 times, another record.

Wahoo Sam also possesses one of the better home-run records—he is the only man to lead both leagues in home runs, hitting 16 with Cincinnati in 1901, and then a modest 7 in 1908 with Detroit and 8 with Detroit in 1914, both good enough to lead the league.

Playing most of his career in the shadow of teammate Ty Cobb, Crawford finished with a .309 lifetime batting average, 2,964 hits, 3 RBI titles (1910, 1914, and 1915), and all those triples.

Tony Oliva

A series of knee injuries curtailed Tony Oliva at the height of his career, but not before the smooth-swinging Cuban outfielder had proven himself one of the finest hitters of the postwar era.

In 1964 the 24-year-old Minnesota Twins slugger became the first rookie ever to win a batting title, with a .323 mark. The average was solidly achieved, too, with 32 home runs, 43 doubles, and a league-leading 217 hits. Proving it was no fluke, Tony came back and led the league again the next year with a .321 average, hitting 40 doubles, knocking in 98 runs, and again leading in hits, with 185.

In 1966 Oliva's average dropped to .307 but he led the league in hits for the third straight time, with 191. Overall, Tony headed the league in hits 5 times and in doubles 4 times. In 1971 he took his third batting crown with a .337 average, his personal high. It was in July of that year that Oliva suffered a severe knee injury while diving for a fly ball in Oakland.

Oliva had suffered knee injuries before and recovered, but not this time. He was forced to sit out virtually the entire 1972 season, and when he came back in 1973 it was strictly as a designated hitter. With a lot of his mobility gone and his ability to pull the ball severely compromised, Oliva never regained the diamond-hard brilliance of his early years. He retired after the 1976 season with a lifetime batting average of .304.

George Foster in 1971

George Foster

For years the front office of the San Francisco Giants was notorious for the poor judgment it showed in player deals. Among the men the Giants traded, with little to show in return, were the three Alou brothers, Gaylord Perry, and Orlando Cepeda. But perhaps the biggest gift of all was outfielder George Foster, whom they traded to Cincinnati on May 29, 1971, for infielder Frank Duffy and a minor-league pitcher.

True, it took Foster several years to assert himself at home plate, but once he did he became the National League's premier pulverizer. Only an injury suffered during the 1979 season, which kept him out of 40 games, prevented him from setting a record that had eluded the game's greatest hitters. Foster had led the league in runs batted in for 3 consecutive years, 1976–1978, sharing the record with the likes of Babe Ruth, Ty Cobb, Honus Wagner, Rogers Hornsby, and Joe Medwick. In his 121 games in 1979 George managed to bat in 98 runs, only 20 less than the leader, Dave Winfield, who played in 159 games for San Diego. Without the injury, Foster would surely have led the league in this most crucial of offensive statistics for an unprecedented fourth consecutive time.

In 1977 and 1978 his 52 and 40 home runs led the league. In 1977, when he was voted the National League's Most Valuable Player, Foster batted .320 and led the league in runs scored with 124, 388 total bases, and a .631 slugging average.

Lefty Grove with the trophy awarded him for being voted the American League's Most Valuable Player in 1931

"Lefty" Grove

Someone once asked catcher Bill Dickey about fastball pitchers.

"I'll tell you about fastball pitchers," Dickey said. "One day we were playing the Athletics in Yankee Stadium. We were behind by one run in the last of the ninth. We loaded the bases with nobody out. Connie Mack signaled his pitcher off the mound and we all looked toward the bullpen to see who was coming in. But nobody was coming in from the bullpen. Grove walked out of the dugout, threw five warmup pitches, then proceeded to fan the side on ten pitches. The last three he threw to me. I haven't seen any of them yet. Don't ever ask me about fastball pitchers again."

Everyone has their favorite Robert Moses "Lefty" Grove story. Most of the stories dwell on Grove's blinding speed, and blinding it must have been, because Lefty, like Walter Johnson, seldom threw a curve. When Grove was pitching everyone knew what was coming, but it didn't matter—that fastball was almost unhittable. And he could throw it for

9 innings, another thing that made Grove the great pitcher he was.

Grove didn't come to the big leagues until he was 25; for several years he pitched for Jack Dunn's independently owned Baltimore club of the International League. Dunn finally sold Lefty to Connie Mack in 1925 for a little more than $100,000, a carload of money then.

Grove and the Philadelphia Athletics of his era were one of those combinations that fans dream about—the mighty pitcher with a hard-hitting team behind him. The record Lefty compiled, aided by the batting thunder of, among others, Jimmie Foxx, Al Simmons, and Mickey Cochrane, has few if any parallels.

In his first 7 years in the American League (1925–1931), Grove led in strikeouts each season. He also led in earned-run average 9 times. (His closest contenders are Grover Cleveland Alexander and Sandy Koufax, both with 5.) His 4 straight ERA titles (1929–1932) is an American League record. He led

in winning percentage 5 times, another record.

Lefty had no peer as a winning pitcher. Take the years between 1928 and 1933. In this 6-year period his won-lost record reads: 24–8, 20–6, 28–5, 31–4, 25–10, 24–8. It adds up to a 6-year record of 152–41, a winning percentage of .788.

In 1931 he won 16 straight games, an American League record he shares with Walter Johnson, Smoky Joe Wood, and Schoolboy Rowe. In his bid for a seventeenth straight win, he lost 1–0 to the St. Louis Browns on a misjudged fly ball. When the temperamental, hard-losing Grove was finished with the Athletics' clubhouse after that game, the place reportedly was in a shambles. Lefty did not like to lose, particularly 1–0 games, and most particularly 1–0 games that ended 16-game winning streaks.

After the 1933 season Mack sold Lefty to the Red Sox. In Boston, Grove posted his eighth and last 20-game season. As time began eroding his great speed, he gradually became a crafty left-hander, crafty enough to win, beginning at age 35, 4 more ERA titles. Midway through the 1941 season, the 41-year-old Grove labored to his three hundredth and final big-league victory. At that time, he was only the fifth pitcher in the modern era to amass that many wins, following Walter Johnson, Grover Cleveland Alexander, Christy Mathewson, and Eddie Plank.

Lefty Grove in spring training before his great 1931 season

Luke Appling

They called Lucius Benjamin Appling "Luke," although there were some American League pitchers who had other names for him. Appling had the knack of being able to foul off 2-strike pitches he did not feel like swinging at, forcing some pitchers to throw to him as many as 10 or 12 times before Luke decided to complete his turn at bat.

This 2-decade shortstop (all 20 of those years spent with the Chicago White Sox) was a marvel with a bat in his hand. He played 15 full seasons and in 13 of them batted over .300. He touched the mountaintop in 1935 when he led the league with a .388 average, the highest figure attained by a shortstop in this century. In his banner year Luke collected 204 hits and drove in 128 runs. In 1943 he won another batting title, hitting .328.

Steady as a rock all through his career, Luke at the age of 42 in 1949 played a full season at shortstop and batted .301. He led shortstops in assists 7 times, a major-league record. His lifetime batting average is .310. Among twentieth-century shortstops only Honus Wagner and Arky Vaughan have done better.

One day Luke asked the White Sox's general manager for a dozen baseballs. The GM said no. Piqued, Appling applied his talents in batting practice and fouled several dozen balls into the stands. Luke was no man to fool with, not for pitchers and not for general managers either.

Three National League outfielders at the 1933 All-Star game in Chicago. Left to right: *Chuck Klein of the Phillies, Chick Hafey of the Reds, Wally Berger of the Braves*

"Chick" Hafey

His contemporaries held Charles "Chick" Hafey in the highest regard, placing the St. Louis Cardinals' outfielder above many others who posted loftier statistics. Hafey was the ballplayer's ballplayer, possessor of the most feared throwing arm in the league, and a fierce right-handed batter whose smoking line drives made life uncomfortable for National League third basemen.

From 1927 through 1932 Hafey put together 6 of the most sweetly consistent seasons of any hitter, ringing up batting averages of .329, .337, .338, .336, .349, and .344. The .349 in 1931 was a league-leading number. It was actually figured out to .3489; it had to be carried to the fourth decimal because Bill Terry's average was .3486 and Jim Bottomley's .3482. It was the tightest race ever for the batting championship.

A winning ballplayer, Chick helped the Cardinals to 4 pennants and 2 world championships over a 4-year period. In the 1939 Series he set a record with 5 doubles.

Sinus trouble forced Hafey to start wearing glasses on the field in 1929, his sixth year in the big leagues. Chick was one of the first players to wear glasses on the field.

A salary dispute with the Cardinals caused him to be traded to Cincinnati in 1932. Hafey played well there, but recurrent sinus problems, plus a shoulder injury in 1935, soon brought this fine ballplayer to premature retirement.

Chick Hafey in 1928

Smoky Joe Wood in 1912

"Smoky" Joe Wood

"Smoky" Joe Wood will always tantalize us. He remains, along with Pete Reiser and Herb Score, one of the great "what ifs" of baseball: what if he had not hurt his arm in the spring of 1913, when he was just 24 years old?

One thing is for certain: the evidence of Joe Wood's greatness is concrete, not speculative. Could the youngster throw as hard as Walter Johnson? Walter himself answered the question in 1912: "Mister, no man alive can throw a baseball harder than Joe Wood." Certainly no one ever threw a ball harder than Wood did in 1912. It was probably the greatest season a pitcher ever had (with the possible exception of Johnson's in 1913). In 1912 the baby-faced Wood won 34 and lost just 5, for a winning percentage of .872 (along the way he won 16 straight). He struck out 258, pitched a league-leading 10 shutouts, and had an earned-run average of 1.91.

In the World Series against the Giants he won 3 more, including the final game against the great Mathewson. The world belonged to young Joe Wood. The following spring, however, he hurt his arm. But even a sore-armed Joe Wood was pretty good. In 1915 he was 15–5, with a league-leading 1.49 earned-run average. Giving up the mound soon after, he ended up in the Cleveland outfield for several years. A fine all-around athlete, Wood batted .366 as a part-timer for the pennant-winning Indians in 1920.

Willie Mays in 1969

Willie Mays

Talking about Willie Mays, we must enlarge the perspective. We are talking about a 50-year ballplayer: that is, one who came up in 1951 and who will probably be the center fielder on everyone's second-half-of-the-century all-star team when that parlor game comes into vogue in the year 1999.

Never was a man more perfectly designed by nature, both in physical endowment and temperament, to play the American game. The Alabama-born innocent could play center field the way poets expected it to be played. He could throw with the might and force of a cannon, he could run as if wind-born, he could hit steadily and with power. And he loved the game the way the fans loved him. With every instinct honed to the bone, he was a dynamic, infectious presence on the diamond, as at home in center field as Olivier on the stage.

In May of 1951 the Giants needed some more punch in their lineup. They had a puncher on their Minneapolis farm club named Mays, hitting a rather conspicuous .477. Willie went hitless in his first few games, and then unloaded his first big-league hit—a long home run off Warren Spahn. The legend was launched. And so were the Giants. With the youngster in center field performing daily heroics with bat and arm and glove, the Giants charged through the season and finally won their "miracle pennant" on Bobby Thomson's home run.

After missing 2 seasons in military service, Willie returned in 1954, older, stronger, and even better. He was the National League's Most Valuable Player that year, hitting 41 home runs, driving in 110 runs, and compiling a league-leading .345 batting average and .667 slugging average.

Mays's versatility was remarkable. Twice he hit over 50 home runs (51 in 1955, 52 in 1965), 4 times he led the league in 4-baggers. He led in triples 3 times and 4 consecutive years (1956–1959) he led in stolen bases. He led in slugging average 5 times, and 3 times in total bases. He hit over 40 home runs 6 times, 10 times he drove in over 100 runs, 12 times he scored over 100 runs. He led National League outfielders in double plays 4 times. In

The catch on Vic Wertz in the 1954 World Series

With Minneapolis in the American Association in 1951

1965 he won a second MVP award. On April 30, 1961, he hit 4 home runs in a 9-inning game, only the fifth man to accomplish this in the twentieth century.

If Willie had not spent the better part of 2 years in the service, it no doubt would have been his home-run record Hank Aaron pursued rather than Babe Ruth's. As it now stands, Mays is third on the all-time list, with 660 home runs.

Willie's most memorable catch occurred in the first game of the 1954 World Series against the Cleveland Indians at the Polo Grounds. With 2 men on base and nobody out in the eighth inning of a 2–2 game, Vic Wertz sent a towering clout out to center field, the ball traveling some 460 feet. Running at top speed with his back to the plate, Willie caught up with the ball and took it over his left shoulder, making one of the most breathtaking catches in Series history. The grab prevented the Indians from scoring and allowed the Giants to go on and win the game in extra innings.

The story is told of the time Giant manager Bill Rigney gathered his young infielders around in spring training to alert them to a certain fact. "When the ball is hit to the guy in center field," Rigney said, "go to a base, because that ball is going to come in where it's supposed to, because Willie knows." There was silence. Then an intrepid youngster asked, "What does Willie know, Skip?" Rigney paused. He apparently had never thought it through. "I don't know what he knows," he said. Then he added firmly and conclusively, "but Willie knows."

The league batting champions getting together before the opening of the 1954 World Series at the Polo Grounds: Bobby Avila of Cleveland (left) *and Willie Mays*

Jimmy Collins in 1903

Jimmy Collins

It was not so long ago that old-timers, those informal historians of the recent past, were telling us that the greatest third baseman who ever lived was Jimmy Collins, whose career ran from 1895 to 1908—most of it played in Boston, first in the National League and then, beginning in 1901, in the American League.

What the old-timers spoke about most admiringly was Jimmy's defensive play, and not even the later play of Pie Traynor could erase the miracles of Collins's glove from their minds. Jimmy was most adept at swooping in and throwing out would-be bunters. In an era when a lot of hitters—including Willie Keeler, Jess Burkett, and Ty Cobb—made a good part of their living by beating out bunts,

this was no small talent. Collins, apparently, played third base the way Hal Chase played first—not just brilliantly but with flair and innovation. The fact that Jimmy was a very early inductee into the Hall of Fame (in 1945, ahead of men like Frank Frisch, Mickey Cochrane, and Traynor himself) indicates the old-timers were keen of eye and sharp of memory when it came to Collins.

Along with the magic in his glove, Collins also had some sting in his bat. From 1900 to 1902 he had batting averages of .304, .332, and .322. His lifetime mark was .294. In 1903 Jimmy was player-manager for the Red Sox and led them into the first World Series ever played, in which Boston beat Pittsburgh.

Al Simmons in 1929

Al Simmons

Al Simmons came out swinging in his rookie year with the Philadelphia Athletics in 1924, and it took American League pitchers 11 years to begin to slow him down. Al, whose unorthodox stance at the plate earned him the name "Bucketfoot," was one of the most lethal right-handed hitters of all time. A prickly personality, he loathed pitchers and accordingly made their lives miserable.

After his first 8 years as an outfielder in the big leagues, his batting average was .364; after 11 years it was .356. In 1925 and 1927 he hit .384 and .392 but was topped each time by Harry Heilmann. In 1930–1931, however, he won back-to-back batting titles with averages of .381 and .390.

He batted in more than 100 runs in each of his first 11 seasons, leading the league with 157 in 1929. He drove in more than 150 runs in a season 3 times, and 6 times he collected more than 200 hits, with a high of 253 in 1925, 4 short of George Sisler's major-league record. Twice, in 1925 and 1929, he led in total bases.

Simmons concluded his big-league career in 1944, finishing as a player-coach with Connie Mack after seeing service with various other clubs. Mack had sold him to the White Sox after the 1932 season, when Connie began dismantling his great 1929–1931 pennant winners. Al's lifetime batting average is .334, achieved with a total of 2,927 hits, including 307 home runs. In 4 World Series, Simmons batted .329 and polled 6 home runs.

Carl Hubbell in 1935

Carl Hubbell

Carl Hubbell, the New York Giants' masterful screwball-throwing left-hander, had many brilliant pitching performances over a 16-year career (1928–1943). But as his record recedes into baseball history, one brief, unforgettable effort remains dominant. It occurred during the second All-Star game, on July 10, 1934, played, appropriately enough, at Hubbell's home field, the Polo Grounds, in New York.

The first 2 batters for the American League, Charlie Gehringer and Heinie Manush, got on base. Settling down and throwing his mystifying screwball, Hubbell proceeded to strike out the next 3 batters—Babe Ruth, Lou Gehrig, and Jimmie Foxx. Then he began the next inning by fanning Al Simmons and Joe Cronin, before Bill Dickey broke the spell with a single. Hubbell's performance remains a landmark effort in baseball history.

Hubbell hit his stride in 1933 when he began reeling off 5 straight 20-game seasons, reaching his peak in 1936 with a 26–8 record. On July 2 of that year he pitched an 18-inning 1–0 shutout against the Cardinals, without walking a single batter. During the 1936–1937 seasons, King Carl won 24 consecutive games.

Overall, the quiet, soft-spoken Hubbell won 253 games. He led the National League in earned-run average 3 times, in wins 3 times, twice in winning percentage, and in 1933 with 10 shutouts.

Ty Cobb (left) *visiting with Christy Mathewson before the third game of the 1911 World Series in New York*

Christy Mathewson

Christy Mathewson was almost too good to be true, any way you look at him. He was big, strong, handsome, intelligent, revered by his teammates, admired and respected by his opponents. He was also, in all probability, the greatest pitcher who ever lived, give a Walter Johnson or take a Grover Cleveland Alexander. He was America's first genuine sports idol, capturing the hearts of fans around the country and especially in New York, where he pitched for the Giants from 1900 to 1916.

Matty worked for John McGraw, his antithesis in every possible respect. McGraw was short, round, tempestuous, profane. By rights they should not have gotten along. But they did. McGraw considered Matty the son he never had and their relationship was warm.

Mathewson attended Bucknell University. He entered pro ball in 1899, was drafted by Cincinnati and then traded to the Giants for Amos Rusie, the greatest pitcher of his day but then over the hill.

In 1901, his first full season in the big leagues, the 21-year-old right-hander won 20 and lost 17. He slumped to 14–17 the next year, but then for the next 12 years never dropped under 22 wins, a record for twentieth-century pitchers. In 1903–1905 his win totals were 30, 33, 31, a feat equaled in modern times only by Alexander. But then Matty scored a fourth 30-victory season in 1908 when he won a monumental 37 games against 11 losses, setting a modern National League record.

Mathewson's earned-run averages are also glories suitable for framing. In 1905 his ERA was 1.27, in 1908 it was 1.43, in 1909 an almost invisible 1.14. He led the league in ERA 5 times, and 5 times he led in strikeouts. His 267 strikeouts in 1903 were remarkably high in an era when few pitchers went over the 200 mark. He led the league in shutouts 4 times, with a high of 12 in the great 1908 season. His 83 lifetime shutouts place him third behind Johnson and Alexander, while his 373 career victories tie him with Alexander for the all-time National League record, a fitting deadlock.

Something else Matty had in common with

Christy Mathewson in 1912

Alexander was pinpoint control. Excellent to begin with, his control got better and better as he went on, to the point where, in 1913, he pitched 306 innings and walked only 21. A year later he walked only 23 in 314 innings.

Mathewson accomplished these pitching marvels on the strength of his control, a good fastball, a curve that broke sharply from the shoulders to the knees, and a pitch then called a fadeaway. The fadeaway was actually a reverse curve, or what is known today as a screwball. As far as available evidence goes, he was the only pitcher of his time to throw this pitch. Matty apparently possessed the most potent pitching arsenal of any hurler who ever lived.

The highlight of this legendary career came in the 1905 World Series, against the Philadelphia Athletics. Mathewson pitched 3 shutouts against the A's in 6 days, allowing just 14 hits and 1 walk while striking out 18 in those 27 unblemished innings. Overall in Series competition he was 5–5, some of his losses coming on unearned runs, as his Series ERA of 1.15 for 102 innings attests.

The steel left Christy's arm rather suddenly, as he dropped from 24 wins in 1914 to an 8–14 record the next year. In 1916 McGraw sent him to Cincinnati, Matty's original team, where Mathewson had been offered the opportunity to manage. He ended his active career that year with a 4–4 record.

On October 7, 1925, the day the World Series opened between Pittsburgh and Washington, Christy Mathewson died of tuberculosis at Saranac Lake, New York. He was 45 years old.

Christy Mathewson soon after his graduation from Bucknell

Tom Seaver

One of the most glittering pitching records in National League history belongs to George Thomas Seaver, the greatest right-hander to work for a New York club since Mathewson. Like Mathewson, the man he idolizes above all pitchers, Seaver is an intelligent, analytical student of the mechanics of pitching, the master of a bewildering variety of pitches.

He joined a downtrodden and hopeless New York Mets club in 1967 and won 16 games in each of his first 2 seasons. In 1969 he and his teammates startled the baseball world by winning the pennant and World Series. Tom's contribution was a 25–7 season, a 2.21 earned-run average, plus a key win over the highly favored Orioles.

It was the first of 5 20-game seasons for him. His major-league records include most seasons with 200 or more strikeouts (10), most consecutive seasons with 200 or more strike-outs (9), most consecutive strikeouts in a game (10), and, a record he shares with Steve Carlton, most strikeouts in a game (19).

His lifetime earned-run average of 2.60 is the lowest of any pitcher in the lively ball era (since 1920). He has led the league in ERA 3 times, strikeouts 5 times, and has won 3 Cy Young Awards (1969, 1973, and 1975).

Because of a contract dispute with the Mets' front office, Seaver was traded to Cincinnati on June 15, 1977, the same club with which Mathewson finished his career.

Three Fingered Brown, circa 1906

"Three-Fingered" Brown

Christy Mathewson's only rival for pitching primacy in the National League in the opening decade of the century was Mordecai Peter Centennial "Three-Fingered" Brown—"Centennial" was because he was born in 1876, "Three-Fingered" was because he lost part of the index finger on his right hand in a corn shredder when he was 7 years old (the little finger was also mangled). This was a case of destiny deciding to mold a pitcher after the fact, because the odd configurations of Brown's fingers enabled him to throw a curveball that had an unusually sharp downward break.

Brown pitched the bulk of his career (1903–1916) for the Cubs, for years arch rivals of the Giants. Brown versus Mathewson was for many seasons the National League's premier gate attraction. In the 24 times these superlative right-handers went to a decision in head-to-head matchups, Brown won 13.

Three-Fingered Brown was simply one of the most difficult pitchers to beat. Over a 4-year period (1906–1909), his winning percentage never went under .750 as he posted records of 26–6, 20–6, 29–9, and 27–9. His highest earned-run average during this period was 1.47, his lowest an unbelievable 1.04 in 1906.

Brown won 20 or more games 6 consecutive years (1906–1911), led the league in shutouts twice, and in earned-run average once. His career record was 208–111.

George Sisler in 1928

George Sisler

George Sisler was called the perfect player. There seemed to be nothing this dazzling left-handed-hitting first baseman could not do on a ball field. He joined the St. Louis Browns in 1915 as a pitcher, but, like another left-hander of the time—Babe Ruth—his career lay elsewhere. The Browns converted George to a first baseman and very quickly he was regarded as the finest fielding first baseman in the league.

It is as a hitter, however, that George Sisler is remembered. The heart of his career came in 1920, 1921, and 1922, when he batted .407, .371, and .420, leading the league in 1920 and 1922. In 1920 he collected 257 hits, the all-time high for a single season. In 1922 his hit total was 246. In each of those sizzling years he drove in more than 100 runs and each year hit 18 triples. In 1921 and 1922 he also led the league in stolen bases. In 1922 he hit in 41 consecutive games, the league record until Joe DiMaggio broke it in 1941.

After the 1922 season a sinus condition which had been plaguing him suddenly worsened and began causing eye problems. He was forced to sit out the entire 1923 season; when he came back, something was missing. There would be later years of batting .345 and .331, but Sisler, a perfectionist and lifetime .340 batter, did not consider this "serious hitting." After 16 seasons he retired in 1930.

For years Sisler was considered the greatest all-time first baseman until, by general consensus, he was replaced by Lou Gehrig.

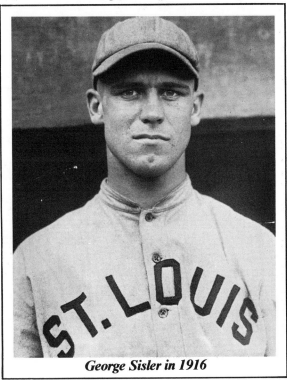
George Sisler in 1916

Lou Gehrig

The story of Lou Gehrig has remained vivid and compelling, more for its tragic elements than its heroic, for the tragedy of Lou Gehrig put the heroics into very poignant perspective. He was "The Iron Horse," the powerful, ruggedly handsome, seemingly indestructible American hero. He was that appealing mix of Herculean strength and shy, quiet modesty that storytellers are loath to put into fiction for fear of straining credulity. He was a sensitive Mama's boy who was wooed away from his domineering mother by a bright, winsome, sophisticated young woman. And above all, he was "The Pride of the Yankees."

He played 2,130 consecutive games for the Yankees—from June 1, 1925, to April 30, 1939—one of the most remarkable records in all of sports history. An ordinary headache had gotten him into the lineup—the afflicted man was first baseman Wally Pipp—and it took a rare, muscle-deteriorating, and fatal disease to finally force him out.

He is one of the few power hitters who can stand comparison with his spectacular team-mate, Babe Ruth. Ruth and Gehrig batting back-to-back in the Yankee lineup for a decade were the most awesome combination in baseball history.

A lifetime .340 hitter, it is Larrupin' Lou's runs-batted-in totals that catch the eye first. For 13 consecutive seasons he drove in more than 100 runs, and in 7 of those seasons he drove in over 150. His 184 RBIs in 1931 is a league record. He also scored more than 100 runs for 13 consecutive seasons.

He hit 493 career home runs, going over 40 5 times. But he was not simply a home-run hitter: he hit scorching line drives in all directions, getting more than 40 doubles 7 times, and 10 or more triples 8 times. He batted above .340 8 times, with a high of .379 in 1930. In 1934 his .363 led the league. His 23 grand-slam home runs is an all-time record. He hit 4 consecutive home runs in a game on June 3, 1932. In the World Series he was devastating, with a remarkable .361 batting average, 10 home runs, and 35 runs batted in in 34 World Series games.

Understandably, he was Manager Joe Mc-

Lou Gehrig, a spectator in the Yankee dugout during the 1939 World Series against Cincinnati

Lou Gehrig and his mother

Carthy's favorite. When it became apparent that he could no longer play (though before it was known that he was suffering from an uncurable illness), McCarthy left him alone. Joe would not take him out of the lineup, a rare and touching tribute to a ballplayer. Finally, on May 1, 1939, in Detroit, Gehrig removed himself. Baffled, frustrated by his body's inability to respond, he went to the Mayo Clinic in Rochester, Minnesota. There, his illness was diagnosed as amyotrophic lateral sclerosis, a disease which atrophies the muscles.

In a poignant Lou Gehrig Day ceremony at Yankee Stadium on July 4, 1939, the dying Gehrig described himself as "the luckiest man on the face of the earth." It was a brave, heartbreaking statement; 2 years later he was dead, 2 weeks short of his thirty-eighth birthday.

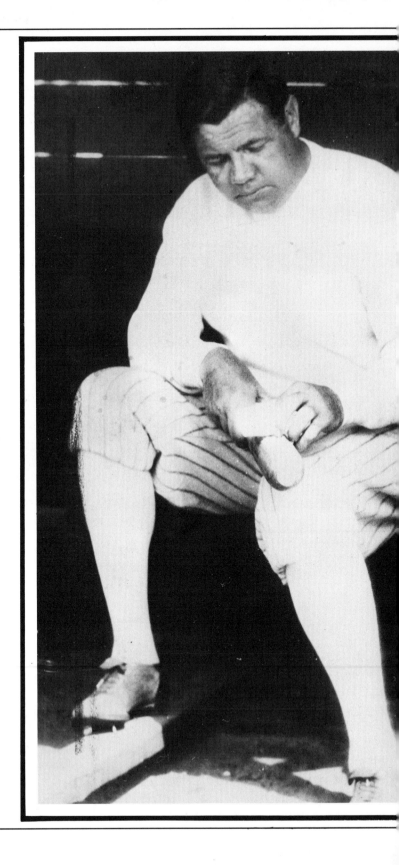

Babe Ruth (left) ***and Lou Gehrig***

Hank Greenberg

In an era of big guns, Detroit's amiable Hank Greenberg set off some of the loudest shots. Contemporary of Babe Ruth, Lou Gehrig, Jimmie Foxx, Joe DiMaggio, and Ted Williams, Big Henry hit with and occasionally outhit the best of them. In 1938 he electrified the baseball world with 58 home runs, tying Jimmie Foxx for the most home runs ever in a single season by a right-handed batter. The year before, he drove in 183 runs, 1 run short of Gehrig's American League record.

The Bronx-born Greenberg had dynamite in his bat. With a lifetime batting average of .313, he led the American League in home runs 4 times and runs batted in 4 times. In 1934 he hit 63 doubles, third highest single season total in American League history. Because of an injury 1 year (1936) and 4½ years in military service, Greenberg's career was limited to 9 full seasons. He nevertheless managed to hit a lifetime total of 331 home runs.

The big first baseman's most dramatic moment came in the last game of the 1945 season. Returning from military service in mid-season, he led the Tigers in a tight pennant race that came down to the last day of the season. Needing the game to clinch the pennant, the Tigers were trailing 3–2 in the ninth inning when Greenberg came to bat with the bases full. Hank promptly unloaded the most explosive home run of his career, giving the Tigers the game and the pennant.

Hank finished his career with the Pirates in 1947 where, according to Ralph Kiner, Greenberg's friendship and batting tips helped the younger man become one of the game's most prolific home-run hitters.

Hank Greenberg in 1939

Jackie Robinson in 1947

Jackie Robinson

No man ever came to major league baseball under greater pressure than Jackie Robinson did with the Brooklyn Dodgers in 1947. Not only was he coming into a highly volatile situation as the first Black player in modern history, not only was he being asked to play an unfamiliar position (first base), but he knew he also had to restrain the tempests of his fiery competitive spirit. Jackie was militant and combative and aggressive. He was all the things anyone would want to see in an athlete. For the first Black man in the big leagues they were all the wrong things.

But Robinson was also an intelligent man, keenly aware of the significance of what he was attempting. It was a tense, dangerous, and lonely crusade. The first man through the color barrier hardly had a crowd at his back: most of the other big-league clubs were on the sidelines, watching Dodger leader Branch Rickey's "experiment" with disapproval and, in some cases, outright hostility.

So Robinson, instructed by Rickey not to fight back, to ignore the taunts and threats and insults, to avoid at all costs any racial incidents on the field, understood what was at stake and was for several years a model of restraint. The cost was high. Unable to give vent to his feelings, Jackie endured what were for him almost unbearable constraints.

But his play did not suffer. He was the athlete supreme, an incomparable competitor, driven by a noble pride. He was the most exciting ballplayer of his time. He was a fine fielder and a deadly clutch hitter, and on the bases he could rattle a pitcher and upset an infield. Daring and defiant but never reckless, he stole home 19 times in his career.

As a 28-year-old rookie in 1947, Jackie hit .297 and led the league in stolen bases. In 1949, his greatest year, he batted a league-leading .342, driving in 124 runs, getting 203 hits, and again leading in stolen bases. He was voted the National League's Most Valuable Player.

Robinson, who would no doubt have come to the big leagues 5 or 6 years earlier had he been white, played 10 years for the Dodgers, hitting over .300 6 times. The versatile Robinson led National League second basemen in fielding 3 times. Besides first and second, Jackie also played third and the outfield for the Dodgers.

His greatest single game occurred on the last day of the 1951 season, when the Dodgers went into extra innings against the Phillies in Philadelphia. Brooklyn needed the game in order to gain a first-place tie with the Giants. In the last of the twelfth Robinson saved the game with a diving 2-out catch of a line drive with the bases loaded. In the fourteenth he won it with a home run against Robin Roberts.

Jackie Robinson will always remain a significant figure in baseball history. Not only was he one of the greatest players ever to play the game, he was also one of its most remarkable men.

Out at second base is the Giants' Whitey Lockman as Robinson throws to first to complete a double play.

Goose Goslin in 1929

"Goose" Goslin

Leon "Goose" Goslin, an awkward, friendly farm boy from south Jersey, came to the big leagues as an outfielder with the Washington Senators in 1921 and immediately established himself as one of the game's premier RBI men. In his first full season, 1923, Goose drove in 99 runs; in 11 of the next 13 seasons he had 100 or more runs batted in.

The left-handed-batting Goslin stung the ball with the sweet consistency of the good hitter. Year in and year out, Goose was there at the end of the season with his sockful of runs batted in—he led the league with 129 in 1924, beating out Babe Ruth—and his solid batting averages. From 1924 to 1927 he hit .344, .334, .354, and .334, and then in 1928 topped it off with a league-leading .379, beating out Heinie Manush by one point on the last day of the season.

Twice Goslin led the league in triples, with 18 in 1923 and 20 in 1925. In 1930 he achieved a personal high of 37 home runs and 138 runs batted in.

In both the 1924 and 1925 World Series he was a terror for the Washington Senators, slamming out a record 6 consecutive hits in 1924 and hitting 3 home runs in each Series. Goose had a golden touch for October money. After being traded to the Browns in 1930, he was traded back to Washington just in time to help the Senators win the pennant in 1933. After the 1933 season he was traded to Detroit, where his hitting was instrumental in winning the pennants in 1934 and 1935. In the 1935 World Series his single in the ninth inning of the sixth game drove in the winning run to give Detroit the World Championship.

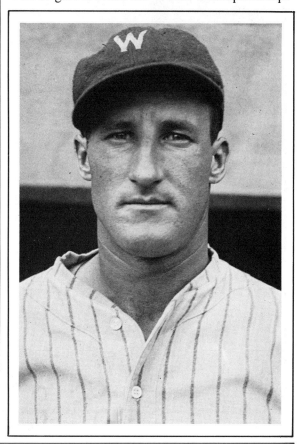

Herb Score in 1955

Herb Score

The inclusion of Herb Score among the game's 100 greatest players can be legitimately questioned, since this gifted left-hander pitched only 2 full seasons before being felled by a savage line drive that struck him flush in the eye. But it is the contention of many that this accident aborted what would have undoubtedly been one of baseball's most scintillating careers.

He joined the Cleveland Indians in 1955; he won 16 and lost 10, striking out 245, still a major-league record for a rookie pitcher. He was even better the next year, winning 20 and losing 9, leading the league again in strike-outs, with 263. It was during the spring of 1957 that the Boston Red Sox startled the baseball world by offering the Indians $1 million for Score. Cleveland resisted the temptation and held onto their young pitcher, whose future seemed unlimited.

Score uncorked his left-handed lightning with such physical force that he was often spun around on the mound after his delivery, left woefully defenseless. Early in the 1957 season he delivered a pitch to the Yankees' Gil McDougald. McDougald lined it directly back at Score. The youngster never saw it. He did not pitch again that year. Though Score gamely tried several comebacks over the next few years, he was never able to recapture the brilliance that had made him, all too briefly, one of baseball's greatest pitchers.

Ty Cobb

A few years ago a sports writer was reminiscing with Ossie Bluege, the fine-fielding former third baseman of the Washington Senators in the 1920s and 1930s. Bluege's German shepherd started barking and despite repeated scoldings would not quiet down. Finally, Bluege raised his voice and said sternly, "Be quiet, Tyrus Raymond!" A moment later a self-conscious grin appeared on the old third baseman's face and he said, almost shyly, "I named him Tyrus Raymond."

Tyrus Raymond Cobb made an impact upon, and left a tangle of memories with, everyone with whom he came in contact on a ball field. No more obsessed, complex, maniacally driven man ever laced on a pair of spikes. Every time at bat was a crusade for Cobb, a violent, tormented, and finally pathetically lonely man. Players who had felt his wrath on the field remembered it so vividly that decades later they would not speak to him, not even at the convivial gatherings of old-timers' games. Cobb, a millionaire through early investment in Coca-Cola stock, once said he would give everything he had if he could only reverse the harsh feelings his old teammates and opponents held toward him.

Ty Cobb in his hotel room, 1912

Ty Cobb at bat with his famous hands-apart batting grip

What would Cobb hit, in terms of batting average, if he were playing today? No one can say for sure, except that it would be enough to lead the league, because, as Paul Richards said, "The drive he had to excel was incredible, and sometimes frightening." For Cobb, above all other players, that drive had life-or-death qualities.

He was a remorseless student of the game, always observing, always asking questions. Blessed with terrific running speed, he used it to full advantage as a deft bunter who frequently rolled his base hits along the foul lines. Using a unique hands-apart grip on the bat, he could place-hit anywhere on the field. He took advantage of Walter Johnson's fear of maiming a batter with a pitch by crowding the plate on him, forcing Johnson to pitch away. He was a terror on the basepaths, often intimidating an infielder or catcher with his ferocious arrivals, spikes high.

It is quite possible that Cobb's personality was warped by a tragic episode that occurred when he was 18 years old. His father, whom Cobb revered, was shot and killed by Ty's mother one night under circumstances never fully explained. The story was that Cobb senior had stealthily entered the house through a window under the suspicion his wife was entertaining another man. Mrs. Cobb claimed she thought she was shooting an intruder.

Whatever accounted for the drive, it was there. Like Babe Ruth's, Cobb's page in the record book is startling. He spent 24 years in the American League, the first 22 with Detroit, the last 2 with the Athletics in 1927 and 1928. In 1927, at the age of 40, he batted .357; the following year, his last, he hit .323.

Cobb stands at the pinnacle with a .367 lifetime batting average, 9 points better than runner-up Rogers Hornsby's. He is the only player in history to amass more than 4,000 hits, with a total of 4,191. His 892 stolen bases were the modern record until eclipsed by Lou Brock in 1977. He stands second in lifetime triples, third in doubles, first in runs scored, and fourth in runs batted in behind power hitters Hank Aaron, Babe Ruth, and Lou Gehrig.

His records are multitudinous. After batting .240 in 41 games as a rookie in 1905 (a figure which must have incensed him), he went on to bat over .300 for the next 23 years. He led the league in batting 12 times, 9 times consecutively (1907–1915). In 1911, he batted .420, the next year .410, the following year .390. In 1917, 1918, and 1919 he took batting titles with averages that stand alone as examples of high-level consistency: .383, .382, .384. In 1922 he hit .401, but came in second to Sisler's .420.

His record of 9 200-hit seasons was finally broken by Pete Rose in 1979. Cobb led the league in hits 7 times, doubles 3 times, triples 4 times, and in home runs once, with 9 in 1909. He led in runs batted in for 3 straight years (1907–1909), a major-league record he shares with several others. He was first in stolen bases 6 times, his 96 thefts in 1915 the 1-season record until broken by Maury Wills in 1962. He led in slugging average 8 times, 6 of those years consecutively (1907–1912). He was baseball's most notable overachiever.

It was Cobb's game and he dominated it with phenomenal exclusivity until 1920, when it became Babe Ruth's game. Cobb's style was to get on base and then use his speed and his guile to outrun a ball or outwit an infielder and score a run. Ruth, with his power—and with a lively ball to boot—would do it with a single stroke and then a nonchalant trot.

Cobb played out his career in Ruth's shadow. But even so, on May 5 and 6, 1925, Cobb accomplished something that not even the mighty Babe ever did—he hit 5 home runs in 2 consecutive games. Having proven some point or other, the 38-year-old Tyrus Raymond, then Detroit's playing manager, went back to his old poke-and-slap style, poking and slapping his way to a .378 average, content to be the lightning to Ruth's thunder.

Lou Brock in 1969

Lou Brock

Lou Brock is the only man to hold both the single-season and career highs in a major category. Roger Maris, for instance, holds the home-run record for a single season, Owen Wilson single-season for triples, Earl Webb for doubles. None of those men is anywhere near the top of the career list in those categories. They enjoyed what amounted to freakish seasons.

There was nothing freakish about out-fielder Lou Brock's accomplishment in 1974, when he broke Maury Wills's record of 104 stolen bases in a season with a staggering 118. Brock had led the National League in swipes in 7 of the previous 8 years, twice going over 70. So it was no great surprise when the Arkansas-born whippet took off at the age of 35 and broke Wills's record.

On his way to an all-time high of 938 lifetime stolen bases, 46 more than Ty Cobb's total, Brock set a record by stealing 50 or more bases for 12 consecutive years. He batted .293 over a 19-year career that began with the Cubs in 1961 and ended with the Cardinals (for whom he played the bulk of the time) in 1979. He hit over .300 8 times, got more than 200 hits 4 times, and in his last season collected his three-thousanth hit, closing out his career with a total of 3,023.

An extraordinary player under pressure, Brock holds the World Series record for highest batting average for a player in 20 or more games (.391). His 14 stolen bases tie him with Eddie Collins for the all-time high in Series competition.

Lou Brock steals base number 893 in San Diego on August 29, 1977, breaking Ty Cobb's lifetime record. Covering the bag is shortstop Bill Almon.

Pie Traynor in 1927

"Pie" Traynor

The saying was, "Twice Hornsby doubled down the left-field line and twice Traynor threw him out." Although Harold "Pie" Traynor was a lifetime .320 hitter, it was his fielding that people preferred talking about—much to Pie's distress, for, like all good hitters, he took great pride in his ability to ride the ball. But Pie was merely another good sticker in a golden age of hitting, whereas at third base he may have been the greatest defensive player ever.

When Traynor had the smooth-fielding Glenn Wright alongside him at shortstop in the 1920s, the left side of the Pittsburgh infield was sealed tight. Pie led National League third basemen in putouts 7 times—a record, as is his lifetime total of 2,288.

No one has ever supplied such a combination of bat and glove at third base as Traynor. He batted over .300 10 times, from 1927 to 1930 ringing up averages of .342, .337, .356, and .366. Though not a home-run hitter, the steady Traynor knocked in more than 100 runs 7 times. In 1923 he led the National League in triples with 19. Sharp-eyed at the plate, Pie struck out only 278 times in a career that ran from 1920 to 1937, fanning only an incredible 7 times in 540 at bats in 1929, one of the lowest full-season figures in the game's history.

Perhaps one day he will be replaced at third base on the greatest all-time team by Brooks Robinson or Mike Schmidt or George Brett. But until that time, the Pittsburgh magician stands alone at the bag.

Pie Traynor (left) *and Ford Frick, then a sports writer, later president of the National League and Commissioner of Baseball*

Luis Aparicio safe at home against the Minnesota Twins. The catcher is Earl Battey.

Luis Aparicio

While the question of who was the greatest defensive shortstop of all time will never be settled, one thing is fairly certain—whoever he is, he is not better than Luis Aparicio. This short, compact Venezuelan went wherever a shortstop had to go, moving with swift, feline grace. No one ever had a surer pair of hands, and few could match the strength and accuracy of his throwing arm.

Luis was remarkably durable during the 18 years he played for the White Sox, Orioles, and Red Sox, appearing in 2,581 games at shortstop (the only position he ever played), the major-league record. For 8 years he led American League shortstops in fielding, a record he shares with Everett Scott and Lou Boudreau. (Luis and Scott did it for consecutive years.) He holds various league records for putouts and assists and double plays for both season and career (he played from 1956 through 1973).

Aparicio was for years the game's premier base-stealer. He led the American League in stolen bases his first 9 years, a league record for times leading and a major-league record for consecutive times leading. Playing in an era when base-stealing was a neglected art, Luis stole over 50 4 times, with a high of 57 in 1964—at that time the second highest number of thefts since 1920.

With his marvelous fielding and dynamic base-running, Aparicio's lifetime batting average of .262 was a decided bonus.

Rube Waddell in 1902

"Rube" Waddell

It has been said that the big, strong, fireballing left-hander George "Rube" Waddell was Connie Mack's favorite among all the players Mack managed during a 53-year career. If the saying is true, there is a certain charm about the firm, businesslike Connie's weakness for his lovable eccentric. The boy never entirely grew out of Rube Waddell, for this powerhouse pitching machine would disappear for days on end during the season to go fishing, or run from the ball park in the middle of a game at the sound of fire bells.

Rube may have been the swiftest lefty of them all. If we choose to judge speed by that fairly dependable gauge, the strikeout, we sees Waddell fanning batters in droves; not only was he on top of the league for 6 straight years (1902–1907), but Rube was sometimes more than 100 whiffs above his nearest competitor. His 349 strikeouts in 1904 (some record books list the number as 343) was an awesome total. It was a figure not even Walter Johnson approached.

From 1902 through 1905, Rube had his big years for Mack, with records of 25–7, 22–16, 25–18, and 26–11. In 1905 he had a league-leading earned-run average of 1.48. His lifetime ERA reads 2.16, his won-lost record 194–141.

In 1907 even the saintly Mack could no longer tolerate Rube's shenanigans and sold him to the Browns. A few years later Waddell was out of baseball. He died of tuberculosis in 1914 at the age of 37.

A view of the Polo Grounds during the 1917 World Series between the New York Giants and the Chicago White Sox

Charlie Gehringer reaching for a high throw at the Detroit Tigers' spring training camp in Lakeland, Florida, March 1939

Charlie Gehringer

Charlie Gehringer had a habit while at bat that gave pitchers a false sense of satisfaction that was followed, usually, by a line drive of rude reality. The Detroit second baseman preferred to hold his bat still until he had 2 strikes. It centered his concentration, he said, and made him a better hitter. The fact that Gehringer struck out as many as 30 times in a season only 3 times in his 19-year career shows that he knew what he was doing at the plate.

They called him "The Mechanical Man." He was the flawless ballplayer, smooth and graceful in the field, leading American League second basemen 9 times in fielding percentage. While his glovework dazzled everyone else, it never particularly impressed Charlie. "You just get that part done," he said, "so you can go back up and hit."

Hit he did. In the 1920s, 1930s, and early 1940s he played 16 full seasons for the Tigers and batted above .300 13 times, with a league-leading .371 in 1937, a mark preceded by years of .354, .330, and .356. He drove in more than 100 runs 7 times, and 12 times he scored over 100. A line-drive hitter, he led the league with 45 doubles in 1929 and with 60 2-baggers in 1936, the fourth highest total in American League history and a figure no one in either league has since topped. He got 200 or more hits in a season 7 times. His lifetime batting average is .320. He was the league's Most Valuable Player in 1937, and without question the greatest second baseman in the last 50 years.

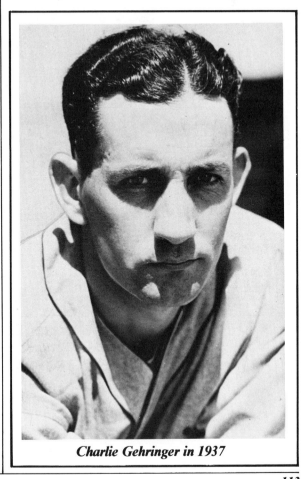

Charlie Gehringer in 1937

Joe Morgan with the Houston Astros in 1965

Joe Morgan

Name it and Joe Morgan has done it.

Fielding? He holds the major-league record for most consecutive errorless games by a second baseman (91). He is tied (with Jerry Adair and Bobby Grich) for fewest errors by a second baseman for a season of 150 games or more (5, in 1977). His .993 fielding average in 1977 is only 3/10 of a percentage point behind Tito Fuentes's National League record.

Base-running? His 625 stolen bases are topped by only three twentieth-century National Leaguers—Lou Brock, Max Carey, and Honus Wagner.

Hitting? Yes, that too. The 5 feet 7 inch, 155-pound Morgan, who reached his peak with Cincinnati in the mid-1970s, batted .327 in 1975 and .320 in 1976, years when he won back-to-back Most Valuable Player awards. Despite his size, Joe hit more than 20 home runs 4 times, led the league in triples in 1971 with 11, and drove in 111 runs in 1976. He scored more than 100 runs 7 times, including 6 years in succession (1972–1977), years when he helped the Reds dominate the National League with 4 division titles, 3 pennants, and 2 World Championships.

Few players have been as versatile as Morgan. He has at one time or another led the league in bases on balls (3 times), slugging average, and sacrifice flies. He is also the first player to steal 60 or more bases and hit 25 or more home runs in the same season, doing it twice (1973 and 1976).

Mel Ott's famous batting style

Mel Ott

It was like something out of the storybooks. A shy, handsome 16-year-old from Gretna, Louisiana, shows up one day at the Polo Grounds in 1925, reporting to John McGraw for a tryout on the recommendation of a Louisiana lumberman. McGraw goes down on the field to watch the boy hit and sees two astonishing things. One is the boy's batting style, totally unorthodox. The young left-handed batter lifted his right foot straight out as the pitcher delivered the ball, then brought it down and swung. That was the second astonishing thing McGraw saw—that swing. It was the sharp, level cut of the natural hitter.

Mel Ott was a natural. And fate had placed him in a most compatible setting, a place where his uncanny ability to pull a ball sharply proved to be lethal, because the Polo Grounds was little more than 250 feet down the right-field line.

Ott played for the Giants from 1926 through 1947, managing the club from 1942 through 1948. Only once in 19 of his first 20 years did he bat under .280. He hit over .300 10 times. Feasting on the cozy right-field stands in the Polo Grounds, he hit 511 home runs (only Ruth and Foxx had more when Ott retired). He led the league 6 times in home runs, and 9 times he drove in more than 100 runs, with a high of 151 in 1929.

Mel Ott was a 16-year-old stranger who came to the big city with a straw suitcase; he remained to become one of the most consistently productive—and popular—players in National League history.

Mel Ott in 1929

Sandy Koufax in 1963

Sandy Koufax

Players of a certain generation will speak with awe about the overpowering speed of Walter Johnson, Lefty Grove, and Bob Feller. There is a kind of pride in their descriptions and impressions of fastballs thrown by these pitchers, as if merely to have batted against them was a privilege, and to have been overmatched by them evidence of their own frail mortality. Johnson, Grove, Feller—a very tight list of larger-than-life pitching aristocrats. In the 1960s it was expanded by one—Sandy Koufax.

In his prime, in the early and mid-sixties, until an arthritic condition in his left elbow forced his retirement at the age of 30, the Los Angeles Dodgers left-hander came close to looking like a professional playing with amateurs. He was that good.

It did not happen quickly for Koufax, however. Signed for a $20,000 bonus by the Brooklyn Dodgers in December 1954, he could not be farmed out because of then-existing rules pertaining to bonus players. Denied the opportunity to learn his craft in the minor leagues, Koufax struggled for 6

Sandy Koufax in 1966

Sandy Koufax in action

years trying to bring his awesome fastball and curve under control. The turnaround came in 1961, when he won 18 and lost 13 and led the league with 269 strikeouts. The next 5 years bordered on the unbelievable: he won 111 and lost 34, a .766 winning percentage.

With 2 of those 5 seasons curtailed by injuries, Koufax's record from 1962 through 1966 was 14–7, 25–5, 19–5, 26–8, 27–9. He won the Cy Young Award as the major leagues' best pitcher 3 times. He set a major-league record by leading in earned-run average for each of those 5 years. In 1965 he set a new major-league record with 382 strikeouts (since broken, by 1, by Nolan Ryan). His 11 shutouts in 1963 were the highest in the league since Grover Cleveland Alexander's 16 in 1916, and an all-time record for a left-hander.

Throwing an almost unhittable curve along with his blinding fastball—with pinpoint control over both—Koufax pitched a record 4 no-hitters (since tied by Ryan), the last of which was a perfect game against the Cubs on September 9, 1965, only the second perfect game in National League history. He holds numerous strikeout records for season, game, and consecutive games.

Koufax, a modest, soft-spoken man, began suffering from circulatory problems in his hand in 1962, problems which were later diagnosed as traumatic arthritis of the left elbow. A tough competitor, he went on pitching for perhaps a year longer than he should have. Often he would have to keep his priceless left arm packed in ice for 30 or 40 minutes after a game. Warned, finally, that continued pitching could eventually cost him use of the arm, Koufax retired after the 1966 season. His lifetime record is 165–87. He averaged better than 1 strikeout per inning over his career, on 97 occasions fanning 10 or more batters in a game.

Whitey Ford, star pitcher for the Thirty-fourth Avenue Baseball Club, receiving a trophy in 1946. Presenting the award is Hall of Fame shortstop Rabbit Maranville.

"Whitey" Ford

When the New York Yankees signed 17-year-old Edward Charles "Whitey" Ford for a $7,000 bonus in 1946, they were getting the man who would eventually become the greatest pitcher in Yankee history

The Yankees' ace through the 1950s and 1960s, Ford never experienced anything even resembling a losing season until the end of his career, which spanned the years from 1950 to 1967. His .690 lifetime winning percentage, built on a 236–106 record, is the highest of any pitcher in this century. His lifetime earned run average was 2.74 for over 3,100 innings pitched with the Yankees.

Brought up in 1950 in the middle of a tight pennant race, Ford broke in with 9 straight wins. After 2 years in the military he returned in 1953 and began his remarkable career in earnest. A product of the sidewalks of New York, Ford was never less than cool, poised, and eminently self-assured on the mound. Master of the breaking pitch, he made batters hit the ball on the ground or lift it into the immense Yankee outfield.

Ford's great years were 1961, when he was 25–4, and 1963, when he was 24–7. Only once between 1950 and 1964 did he lose as many as 10 games in a season. Whitey's pride of performance came in the 1960 and 1961

World Series, when he pitched 33⅔ scoreless innings against the Reds and Pirates, including 3 shutouts. The pitcher whose World series scoreless innings record he broke was another left-hander—Babe Ruth.

Whitey Ford (left) *and fellow Yankee left-hander Bobby Shantz*

Ernie Banks in 1953

Ernie Banks

For almost 20 years Ernie Banks was possessor of one of the sweetest dispositions and meanest bats in the National League. The man who was known as "Mr. Sunshine" hit 512 home runs in his 19-year career (1953–1971) with the Chicago Cubs, tying him with Eddie Mathews for fourth place on the all-time National League list.

The amiable Banks played in the Cubs' infield for 19 years, the first 9 at shortstop, the remainder at first base. Tall and lean, Banks generated tremendous power, whipping a comparatively light 31-ounce bat with a pair of the strongest wrists in baseball.

Banks was one of those long-term Chicago players—Luke Appling and Ted Lyons of the White Sox are two others—who never made it to the World Series, which forced him to settle for personal achievements. Among these are the all-time single-season record for home runs by a shortstop, 47, in 1958, one of 5 times he hit more than 40 home runs in the late 1950s and early 1960s. Leading the league in home runs in 1958, he came back to lead again in 1960 with 41. He also topped the National League in runs batted in in 1958 and 1959, the first National League shortstop since Honus Wagner in 1909 to lead in RBIs. The 1958 and 1959 seasons represent the peak of Banks' career, for he was voted the league's Most Valuable Player in each of those years, the first man in National League history to win the award in back-to-back years (Joe Morgan has since become the second).

Stan Musial

Stan Musial was the National League's greatest slugger since Rogers Hornsby. Like Hornsby, Musial came to the major leagues with the St. Louis Cardinals; but unlike Hornsby, "Stan the Man" spent his entire career with St. Louis, all 22 years of it.

Musial joined the Cardinals at the tail end of the 1941 season, having been converted from sore-armed pitcher to outfielder. Playing 12 games at the end of a tough pennant race, Stan hit .426, giving the league a taste of things to come.

In several important respects, Musial was extremely fortunate in his career. For one thing, he lost only 1 year (1945) to military service. For another, his career was virtually injury free (between 1943 and 1956 he missed only 24 games). And he played in a ball park with a right field that was most accommodating to his left-handed swing. Utterly devoid of star temperament, he was congenial, pleasant, and universally admired and respected.

Musial's page in the record book, like Babe Ruth's, Lefty Grove's, and Ty Cobb's, calls for framing. His lifetime batting average is .331, with 3,630 lifetime hits, second only to Ty Cobb and Hank Aaron. His 725 doubles are second only to Tris Speaker's 793. He won 7 batting titles. He led the league in hits 6 times, 8 times in doubles (a major-league record he shares with Honus Wagner and Tris Speaker), 5 times in triples (a National League record), 6 times in slugging, and 6 times in total bases. For 16 consecutive seasons he batted over .300, with highs of .376 in 1948 and .365 in 1946.

Hal Chase, about 1910

Hal Chase

Hal Chase remains one of baseball's most intriguing characters. He is remembered as one of the game's most brilliant performers, a defensive wizard at first base for the New York Yankees (then known as the Highlanders) from 1905 to 1913, when he was traded to the White Sox. His contemporaries claimed he was the greatest fielding first baseman of all time, an assertion that must be taken on faith today. No doubt he was one of the best. Evidently Chase, who batted right-handed but threw left, was a pioneer in playing away from the bag, and the sight of him cutting off would-be base hits to right field, scrambling to the bag with great agility, and throwing to second base for force outs, must have made quite an impression at the time.

Chase is also remembered as one of the game's most unsavory characters. He was known to have associated with gamblers and was frequently suspected of turning his energies toward helping his opponents along now and then, and not out of any sense of sportsmanship. Roger Peckinpaugh, later a stellar shortstop for the Yankees and Senators, was a youngster in 1913 with the Yankees. His recollection of Hal Chase:

"I remember a few times I threw a ball over to first base, and it went by him to the stands and a couple of runs scored. It really surprised me. I'd stand there looking, sighting the flight of that ball in my mind, and I'd think, 'Jeez, that throw wasn't that bad.' Then

Hal Chase with Cincinnati in 1916

I'd tell myself that he was the greatest there was, so maybe the throw was bad. Then later on when he got the smelly reputation, it came back to me, and I said, 'Oh-oh.' What he was doing, you see, was tangling up his feet and then making a fancy dive after the ball, making it look like it was a wild throw."

Along with his great fielding prowess, Chase was an adequate hitter, with a lifetime .291 batting average. He hit over .300 5 times, his .339 mark leading the National League in 1916, when he was playing for Cincinnati.

Chase's reputation became increasingly malodorous as the years went on. With baseball lacking a strong central authority at the time, the fact of Chase's associating with gamblers and the suspicion that he was betting on and even throwing games was not acted upon. Surprisingly, Chase's last year in the big leagues, 1919, was spent with the Giants under John J. McGraw. What could McGraw have thought about his shady first baseman and did "Prince Hal" ever allow any good throws to go skipping by with men in scoring position?

It is strongly believed that Chase was involved as a go-between for the gamblers and the White Sox players who threw the 1919 World Series to Cincinnati. When Judge Landis took over as baseball's commissioner in 1920, Chase was finished in the major leagues, although never formally barred. Significantly, Prince Hal, no doubt a realist, left without a protest. He was 36 at the time, probably with a few good years left.

An intriguing thought: in 1918 Chase was traded from Cincinnati to the Giants. If Hal had remained with the Reds, he would have played in the 1919 Series against the White Sox. Given the nature of his reputation, no doubt somebody would have approached him with a deal to throw the Series to the White Sox, while the White Sox were at the same time busy throwing it to the Reds. It could have made for one sloppy World Series.

Warren Spahn in 1958

Warren Spahn

Most of the time the phrase "poetry in motion" is simply sports-writing hyperbole, better applied to a copy of Tennyson thrown out the window. But wrap the label on Warren Spahn and you have something. This left-hander was classic: he was smooth, graceful, fluid; he was, in fact, poetry in motion.

Spahn was blessed with one of the most resilient arms in baseball history. From 1947 (his first full year with the Braves) through 1963, he started between 32 and 39 games every season. And he had a knack of finishing what he started, leading the National League in complete games 9 times, including 7 consecutive years (a record) from 1957 through 1963—his last season.

Because of 3 years in the military service, Spahn didn't get started until 1946, when he was 25. Nevertheless, pitching until 1963, he won 363 games, a total topped in this century only by those Olympians Johnson, Mathewson, and Alexander. He won 20 or more games in a season 13 times, tying with Mathewson for the modern record. He led the league in wins 8 times, also a record. His 63 lifetime shutouts place him sixth on the modern list. He also led 3 times in earned-run average, 4 times in strikeouts, 3 times in shutouts, and pitched 2 no-hitters, the second one 5 days after his fortieth birthday.

His best seasons were 23–7 records with Milwaukee in 1953 and again in 1963 when he was 42 years of age.

Boston Braves manager Billy Southworth watching his star pitchers, Warren Spahn (left) and Johnny Sain

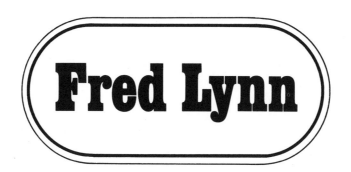

Fred Lynn

Fred Lynn came into the American League in 1975 with one of the most explosive rookie seasons on record, winning an unprecedented double honor—Rookie of the Year and Most Valuable Player. He had warmed up at the end of the 1974 season by batting .419 in 15 games.

Making a most indelible entrance to the big leagues, the Red Sox center fielder batted .331, hit 21 home runs, drove in 105 runs, and set a mark for rookies with his 47 league-leading doubles. He also topped the league in slugging average with .566. In the bargain, Lynn proved himself an extraordinarily gifted center fielder, with his outfield play one of the highlights of the "greatest World Series ever" that October between Boston and Cincinnati. On the road to greatness in 1975 Fred had a special night for himself in Detroit on June 18, when he hit 3 home runs and tied a league record with 16 total bases.

Lynn followed his great season with a .314 encore in 1976, lost some of his edge to injuries the next 2 seasons, then roared back in 1979 to lead the American League in

batting with a .333 average and again in slugging with a .637 mark. He hit 39 home runs, 42 doubles, and drove in 122 runs, while continuing his exciting play in center field.

Only 29 years old going into the 1981 season, Lynn is a man who can do it all on a baseball field and shows every indication of doing it better and better as time goes on.

Fred Lynn (left) ***and Jim Rice***

Home Run Baker in 1911

"Home Run" Baker

John Franklin "Home Run" Baker was one of the American League's first big bombers, although his home-run totals look absurdly meager by today's standards. Nevertheless, Baker did lead the league in home runs 4 consecutive years, 1911–1914, with totals of 9, 10, 12, and 8. It was an age when there was no such thing as the home-run trot, not only because so few were hit but because many that were hit were inside-the-park jobs. The home-run dash preceded the home-run trot.

Baker was the third baseman in Connie Mack's famed "$100,000 infield," which included Stuffy McInnis at first base, Eddie Collins at second, and Jack Barry at shortstop. Baker earned his nickname in the 1911 World Series. In the second game against the Giants he hit a home run that beat Rube Marquard, 3–1. In a ghost-written newspaper column, Marquard's teammate Christy Mathewson criticized Rube for getting "careless" with Baker. The next day Baker hit a game-tying ninth-inning home run against Matty, a game the A's went on to win in the eleventh inning. The next day Marquard twitted Mathewson in *his* ghosted column. The flap earned Home Run Baker what is probably the most high-sounding nickname in baseball.

Baker's top years coincided with his home-run crowns, when he batted .334, .347, .336. and .319. In 1912 and 1913 he led the league in runs batted in with 133 and 126. He also hit a league-leading 19 triples in 1909 and another 21 3-baggers in 1912. He actually hit more triples than home runs, but nobody ever thought of calling him Three Bagger Baker.

"Babe" Ruth

Once upon a time there lived in the city of New York a man named George Herman Ruth. People called him "Babe." He was a big man, with a large, happy smile. Babe traveled around the country a great deal and wherever he went huge crowds of people paid money to see him, because he brought them joy and excitement. People said he could hit a baseball so high it would strike a cloud and cause rain to pour, and so far that the human eye could not follow it. It was said that his smile could chase away the dark and make the sun shine, and that with a wink of his eye he could make a sick child well again. It has been written that he once pointed to a distant spot and then proceeded to drive a baseball to that place. It has been said that he could eat 25 hot dogs at a sitting and then settle them with one mighty belch. It has been said that he saved baseball after the scandal of the 1919 World Series, and that at one time the three most famous Americans in the world were George Washington, Abraham Lincoln, and Babe Ruth.

Myths have accumulated around the Babe like rings around Saturn. It is too late now to sort them all out and only a cold-hearted historian would want to try. Accept him for what he was. Look at that great smiling face and try to deny that its owner was not capable of working miracles.

He may not have saved baseball—the question is debatable—but he certainly brought it into a new era, an era of unparalleled excitement, big money, and national consciousness. His prodigious distance-hitting has never been equaled and probably never will be, because Ruth was physically unique, possessed of a rare combination of lightning reflexes, superb judgment and timing, and excellent eyesight.

Son of a Baltimore saloon keeper, brought up mostly in a school for wayward boys, he began as a left-handed pitcher for the Red Sox in 1914. Between 1915 and 1918 he won 78 and lost 40, never had an earned-run average over 2.44, and led the league in 1916 with 1.75, 9 shutouts, and a 23–12 record. He was 24–13 the next year. He was 3–0 in World Series competition, with an 0.87 ERA for 31

innings, and pitched 29⅔ scoreless innings, a Series record until Whitey Ford broke it in 1961. In 1918 he alternated between pitching and the outfield and led the league with 11 home runs and a .555 slugging average.

A full-time outfielder the next year (1919), he set a new home-run record with a then astonishing 29, also leading the league again in runs batted in and slugging average. In 1920 he was sold to the Yankees by a Red Sox owner who needed money to finance his theatrical ventures (the owner, Harry Frazee, didn't know he had just sold the greatest show on earth for $125,000).

Ruth was a rare case of the man matching the athlete's feats. The Babe had a gargantuan personality to go with his mammoth home run record and his voracious appetites, which included just about every gratification of flesh known to man. He was a lusty eater and drinker and, by all reports, a grand-scale womanizer.

And, yes, the statistics. Like a recitation of virtues, they are so remarkable that they sound monotonous. He remains the all-time home-run champion, and never mind Hank Aaron. He led or tied for the lead 12 times, with peaks of 60 in 1927, 59 in 1921, 54 in 1920, 54 in 1928. (How many people have you ever encountered who hit over 50 in a season 4 times?) He led in runs batted in 5 times, with a high of 171 in 1921.

A closer look at that 1921 season is rewarding. If anyone asks you what was Babe Ruth's greatest season, take a chance and say 1921. He hit 59 home runs (for the third year in a row setting a new 1-season home-run record.) Of every 8 home runs hit in the American League that year, 1 was hit by Babe Ruth. He drove in 171 runs and scored 177, an all-time high. He walked 144 times. He hit 44 doubles and 16 triples, amassed a record 457 total bases, and batted .378. His slugging average was .846 (the year before it was .847, and if you don't think those are some potatoes, consider that no hitter in history, except Ruth himself, has ever come within 100 points of either figure). It was the single most sustained performance of devastation in baseball history.

He hit above .370 6 times, with a high of .393 in 1923. His lifetime batting average is .342. His lifetime slugging average is .690, 56 points higher than that of runner-up Ted Williams. If you don't think pitchers feared him, note that during the 8 years between 1926 and 1933 he led the league in bases on balls 7 times, despite the fact that he had Gehrig hitting behind him all the time.

His single most famous time at bat came in

He would accommodate virtually any request a photographer made.

the third game of the 1932 World Series against the Cubs in Wrigley Field. Under a brutal tirade from the Cub bench jockeys, he took 2 strikes, then looked over at the Chicago dugout and made some sort of gesture—no 2 versions of this fable are alike—and then pickled the next pitch and drove one of the most ferocious home runs of his life. Later it was said that the gesture had been a pointing to where he would hit the ball, and Ruth, showman that he was, went along with it. The story grew; it was too good not to be true, and anyway it was the kind of thing a legend would do.

After 15 years with the Yankees, Ruth was released to the Boston Braves in February 1935. He played in 28 games for the Braves, then retired several days after one last, almost defiant demonstration of his might—hitting 3 titanic home runs at Forbes Field in Pittsburgh on May 25.

Wasted by cancer, the legend, now a mere mortal once more, died in New York City on August 16, 1948, at the age of 53.

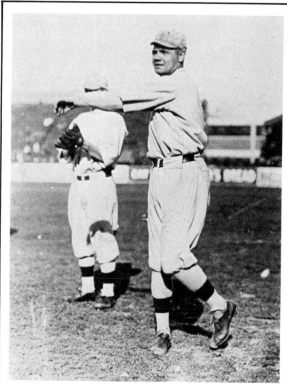

Left-handed pitcher Babe Ruth of the Boston Red Sox, 1916

Babe Ruth in 1922

Ruth hitting a World Series home run against the Cardinals on October 6, 1926, one of 3 he hit that day. The catcher is Bob O'Farrell.

Hank Aaron hitting number 500 on July 14, 1968

Hank Aaron

There are certain parallels between the careers of Hank Aaron and Stan Musial. Each was blessed with a marvelous and durable physique, enabling him to go through a 20-year career without missing appreciable numbers of games. Each was relatively injury free. Where Musial missed only 1 year to military service, Aaron missed none. And each slugged away with a consistency that was businesslike and efficient.

Murderously consistent, Aaron was never dominant. He never won the Triple Crown, his highest batting average was .355 (the only time he hit over .328), his greatest RBI total 130, and his highest home run total 47.

But Hank did hit those 755 home runs. Between 1955 and 1973 he never hit fewer than 24 nor more than 47. He hit more than 40 homers 8 times, drove in more than 100 runs 11 times, batted over .300 14 times. He simply kept at it with a methodical, high-level pace and ended up first on the all-time list in games played, at bats, home runs, and runs batted in; second in hits and runs scored; and sixth in doubles.

Aaron won 2 batting titles, in 1956 (.328) and 1959 (.355). He led the league in hits twice, doubles 4 times, home runs 4 times, runs batted in 4 times, slugging average 4 times. He was a fine defensive outfielder—

playing right field most of the time—and a good base-runner. But most of all he just kept swinging, swinging away, one stroke at a time, until he reached the top.

Ed Walsh in 1909

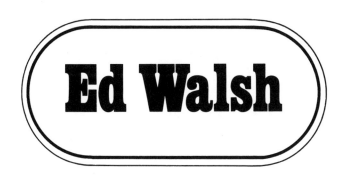

Ed Walsh

Ed Walsh was one of the great spitball pitchers of all time, and thus by definition one of the greatest of all pitchers. Big Ed, as he was known (he stood 6 feet 1 inch and in those days anyone that tall was usually called "Big"), pitched for the White Sox from 1904 until 1916, although 1912 was his last year as a regular starter.

In 1908 Walsh was practically a 1-man band on the mound for the White Sox. He started 49 games, completed 42 (he relieved 17 times, too, just to keep busy on his days off), and wound up with a record of 40–15 (that's right, 40 wins). He pitched 464 innings that year (a modern record), walked only 56, struck out 269, pitched 12 shutouts, and logged a 1.42 earned-run average.

Walsh's spitball—old-timers say he prac-

tically invented the pitch—must have ridden the sweet, turn-of-the-century summer afternoons like a roller coaster. His earned-run averages between 1906 and 1910 read: 1.88, 1.60, 1.42, 1.41, and 1.27. Those are impressive. Even more impressive is that in 1910, when he had his 1.27 ERA, Ed had a losing record—18–20. He was pitching for a club known as the Hitless Wonders, and in that 1910 season the White Sox batted a harmless .211 and hit only 7 home runs. Walsh thus achieved the somewhat miraculous feat of leading American League pitchers in both earned-run average and games lost.

Twice Walsh won 27 games, once 24, and 195 in all. His 1.82 lifetime ERA is the lowest in major-league history.

Addie Joss in 1910

Addie Joss

Hall of Fame rules stipulate that a man must have appeared in at least parts of 10 seasons in order to be eligible for entry. Addie Joss played only 9 years (1902–1910), but in 1978 the Committee on Veterans bent a rule for Addie, being unable any longer to overlook his glittering 1.88 lifetime earned-run average, second on the all-time rolls only to Ed Walsh's 1.82. Also taken into consideration was the fact that it was no fault of Addie's that he did not play beyond his ninth year, since he died on April 14, 1911, at the age of 31, on the eve of his tenth season. His death was caused by complications related to tubercular meningitis.

Joss threw a good fastball and an exceptionally sharp curve. His earned-run averages don't seem real—5 times he was under 2 runs a game, and in 1908 his ERA was 1.16 for 325 innings of work. That was the year he engaged Ed Walsh in one of the game's most memorable pitching duels, on October 2, 1908. Joss's Cleveland team and Walsh's White Sox were locked in a 3-way race for the pennant with Detroit (the Tigers eventually won). Walsh pitched a 4-hitter, striking out 15, and allowing only 1 run. However, 1 run seemed to be enough for Joss most days, and it certainly was on this day: he pitched a perfect game—27 up, 27 down.

Joss won 20 games 4 times, with a high of 27 in 1907. Another of his remarkable statistics is 261 games started and 235 completed.

Pete Reiser

The Cardinals began scouting him when he was 12 years old. Branch Rickey considered him the greatest young player he had ever seen. Leo Durocher thought Willie Mays "might" have been better. The player in question was Harold "Pistol Pete" Reiser.

Of all the careers aborted by injuries, Pete Reiser's may well have been the greatest. The St. Louis–born youngster not only could do it all on a baseball field, but he was also born with the great intangible that no coach or manager can teach a boy—that zealous desire to compete and excel, which in Reiser rose to blazing heights. This desire, blended with his white-hot natural abilities, electrified the National League in 1941, his first full season with the Brooklyn Dodgers. The 21-year-old center fielder won the batting crown with a .343 batting average, and also led the league with 39 doubles, 17 triples, 117 runs scored, and a .558 slugging average.

He could hit from either side of the plate and throw with either hand. He could play infield or outfield. No one could outrun him. He had power, generated by a short, savage swing.

Liberated by Judge Landis from the sprawling Cardinal farm system because of manipulative practices by the St. Louis organization, Reiser signed with Brooklyn in 1938 for a $100 bonus. He showed up in the Dodgers' spring training camp in 1939, a total unknown. The youngster broke into exhibition games with a detonation, getting on base his first 11 times at bat, including home runs against Lefty Gomez and Tommy Bridges. Brooklyn manager Leo Durocher could not believe what he was seeing.

In 1941 Pete proved he was for real, and in 1942 he was doing even better. In mid-July he was batting close to .390 and climbing. And then in St. Louis, while chasing a fly ball hit by Enos Slaughter, he ran flush into the concrete wall in center field.

Reiser's collision with the wall resulted in a fractured skull and a deep concussion. Doctors recommended the youngster not play anymore that season. Durocher, however, was in the midst of a pennant race, and soon he unwisely reinserted Reiser into the lineup. Pete suffered dizzy spells and double vision, and his batting average dropped to .310 by

Pete Reiser safe at home

season's end. By his own admission, he cost the Dodgers the pennant.

After the 1942 season Pete went into the army for 3 years. When he returned in 1946 he was bedeviled once more by injuries. There seemed to be no end of them: beanings, pulled muscles, broken bones, jarring collisions with fences. But the drama and the excitement and the daring never left him, and in 1946 he stole home a record 7 times.

In 1947 he started off healthy once more, but one June night at Ebbets Field he again ran headlong into the center-field wall. This time he almost died. He was virtually paralyzed for 10 days. Nevertheless, he returned later in the season, batted .309, and helped the Dodgers to the pennant. In the World Series against the Yankees, a hard slide into second base broke a bone in his ankle. Then, in the historic fifth game, when Yankee

September 1946: Pete Reiser is being carried off the field after breaking his ankle in a play at first base. Helping out along with the trainer are Vic Lombardi (number 18), Rex Barney (number 26), and Cookie Lavagetto (number 5).

pitcher Bill Bevens had a no-hitter going into the last of the ninth, 2 managers paid supreme tribute to Pistol Pete. Dodger manager Burt Shotton sent Reiser, with a cast on his ankle, up to bat with the tying run on second. Yankee manager Bucky Harris chose not to pitch to him—broken ankle or no broken ankle—and put the winning run on base. A moment later Cookie Lavagetto won it for the Dodgers with his dramatic pinch-hit double.

In 1948 the long and relentless pounding of injuries finally showed on the 29-year-old Reiser. He batted .236. The Dodgers traded him; he shuffled about with several teams, trying to rekindle that precious flame, but was unable to do so. In a few years he was gone from the big leagues, leaving behind a legend special unto itself.

Mickey Cochrane in 1931

"Mickey" Cochrane

Perennial candidate for the greatest catcher of all time, Gordon Stanley "Mickey" Cochrane was the galvanizing force on 2 outstanding championship ball clubs, the 1929–1931 Philadelphia Athletics and the 1934–1935 Detroit Tigers (which the fiery catcher also managed).

Along with his multiple skills behind the plate and with the bat, his contemporaries talk about Cochrane's ruggedness and his leadership qualities. A vigorous, hard-driving scrapper, Mickey's lifetime batting average of .320 is the highest ever recorded by a catcher. In the A's pennant-winning seasons, he batted .331, .357, and .349. In 4 other seasons he batted .320 or better. Unusually fast for a catcher, he often batted second in Connie Mack's lineup.

In 1934 Mack sold him to the Tigers, where Cochrane, then 31 years old, took over as manager as well as catcher. Winning pennants in his first 2 years in Detroit, Cochrane's Tigers brought Detroit its first World Championship in 1935.

On May 25, 1937, Cochrane came to bat at Yankee Stadium. The Yankee pitcher was Irving "Bump" Hadley. The count went to 3 balls and 1 strike. Hadley delivered a high, sailing fastball. Cochrane lost track of it for a split second, then never picked it up again.

The ball crashed against his head with sickening impact, fracturing his skull in 3 places. Lingering near death for several days, Cochrane gradually recovered. But his playing days were over.

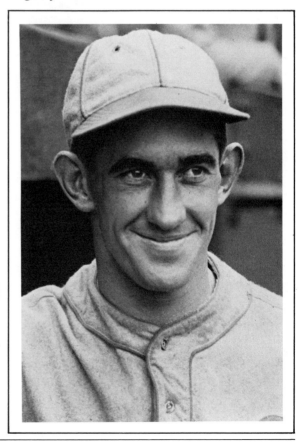

Dave Parker about to score as Montreal's Gary Carter awaits the throw, September 1975. Yes, Carter survived.

Dave Parker

Pittsburgh's 6-feet 5-inch 230-pound right-fielder is a man of supreme self-confidence, the kind of self-confidence that begins quietly with faith in his talent and goes on to pride in his accomplishments. Among Dave Parker's accomplishments are a Most Valuable Player Award in 1978 and 2 consecutive batting titles, in 1977 (.338) and 1978 (.334). He has also taken 2 slugging titles, in 1975 and 1978, and led with 215 hits in 1977 and 44 doubles the same year.

Parker's goals, however, are high and long-range. He hopes to collect 3,000 hits and win a Triple Crown before he retires. Coming from almost any other player, these aspirations might seem naïve and unrealistic. No one in baseball, however, doubts the talents and capabilities of the powerful Pirate. Since becoming a regular in 1975, he has hit over .300 5 consecutive times. And despite leading National League outfielders several times in errors, Parker is considered as skilled on defense as he is on offense, with great quickness for a big man and with one of the finest throwing arms in baseball (he led with 26 assists in 1977).

The year 1972 was the late Roberto Clemente's last season; 1973 was Dave Parker's first. Somebody up there, it seems, has a fondness for right field in Pittsburgh.

Comiskey Park, Chicago, in the mid-1950s

Iron Man McGinnity in 1906

"Iron Man" McGinnity

In an era when pitchers consistently worked over 300 innings, Joe McGinnity was known as "Iron Man." The powerfully built right-hander, who snapped off an underhand curveball that apparently placed a minimum of strain on his arm, came by his nickname honestly. In 1903 Joe pitched 434 innings for John McGraw's Giants, a modern National League record. The year before he worked 382 innings, and a year later 408.

In 1903 he started 48 games and completed 46. He was 31–20 that year. His biggest year was 1904, when he was 35–8. With teammate Mathewson winning 30 and 33 in those years, they made a remarkable pitching twosome. In 1904 McGinnity posted a 1.61 ERA for his 408 innings.

The records aren't quite clear as to just when McGinnity first was called Iron Man, but August 1903 would have been as good a time as any. For it was in that most sultry and ennervating month that Joe, on August 1, 8, and 31, pitched and won *both* ends of a doubleheader. This stands as a record for gallantry, stamina, and foolhardiness.

McGinnity pitched in the big leagues from 1899 to 1908, only 10 years, but given his spirit it was long enough to compile a 247–145 record. Lest anyone think his arm fell off in 1908, it should be noted that Joe was still pitching minor-league ball as late as 1925, at the age of 54. Iron, it seems, does not wear out.

Rogers Hornsby

Those who knew him describe Rogers Hornsby as having the coldest gray eyes they had ever seen. If he had been born earlier, perhaps this Texas boy would have been a gunfighter instead of the greatest right-handed hitter who ever lived.

Hornsby joined the Cardinals at the end of the 1915 season, and 2 years later he was hitting .327, leading the league in triples and taking the first of his 9 slugging titles. (Little-known fact: in 1917–1918 the greatest second baseman of all time was the Cardinals' regular shortstop.)

Rogers, a cold, brutally frank man (some people appreciated his unvarnished candor, others hated him for it), could stop the show just by taking batting practice. Only 2 other hitters—Ted Williams and Babe Ruth—have been able to mesmerize their peers simply by picking up a bat.

In 1920 Hornsby warmed up with his first batting title, hitting .370. It looked good at the time, but the Rajah himself would make it look anemic for the next 5 years. By rights

he could have been arrested for assault and battery upon National League pitchers from 1921 to 1925, when he lit up the skies with consecutive batting averages of .397, .401, .384, .424, and .403, an average of .402 for the 5 years.

Hornsby led the league in hits 4 times (205 in 1922), doubles 4 times, triples twice, home runs twice, runs scored 5 times, and batting 7 times. He hit over .380 8 times.

In 1926, player-manager Hornsby led the Cardinals to their first pennant and then a World Series upset of the Yankees. He then demanded from his employer a 3-year contract at $50,000 a year. This was too much for the flinty soul of owner Sam Breadon, who promptly swapped his popular star to the Giants for Frank Frisch and pitcher Jimmy Ring. Understandably, Cardinal fans were upset, but Frisch's great play soon mollified them.

The outspoken Hornsby was never easy to get along with. He hit .361 for the Giants and was traded after 1 year to Boston; he hit .387

Rogers Hornsby and Babe Ruth during the 1926 World Series

for Boston and was traded after 1 year to the Cubs, where he became player-manager in 1930.

He was in some ways an eccentric. He refused to go to the movies and never read anything but the racing form (which he perused diligently), for fear he would strain his incomparable eyesight. But we must forgive .400 hitters their quirks and foibles, for they are, after all, unique.

Along with his lifetime batting average of .358 (second only to the unique Ty Cobb), Hornsby was a good fielder and in his prime could run as well as anyone. Outside of baseball and the ponies, he seemed to have few interests. Golf? "When I hit a ball," said Rogers, "I want somebody else to chase it."

"Dazzy" Vance

His name was Clarence Arthur Vance but he was known as "Dazzy" and he did not win his first big-league game until he was 31 years old. The big, strong, high-kicking, hard-throwing right-hander had been bouncing around the minor leagues for 10 years when he joined the Brooklyn Dodgers in 1922. A combination of a bad arm and occasional spells of wildness kept Vance down on the farm for a decade.

Like Bob Feller, Vance threw a wicked curve along with his hard one. He was the National League's premier pitcher in the 1920s, winning more than 20 games 3 times. His greatest season was 1924, when he was 28–6, leading the league in earned-run average with a 2.16 mark, in strikeouts with 262

(over 100 more than the runner-up), and completing 30 of 34 starts. If you don't think Dazzy impressed the league that year, he was voted its Most Valuable Player—and that was the year Hornsby batted .424.

Vance holds the National League record for consecutive years leading in strikeouts—7—which he achieved in his first 7 years in the league. Despite his late arrival in the big time, he went on to win 197 games.

A colorful, genial character, Vance was a gifted storyteller who often told a good one on himself. He was the man whose fouled-up base-running was responsible for those 3 Brooklyn Dodgers ending up on third base in a game in 1926, for which Babe Herman has been catching opprobrium ever since.

Ross Youngs in 1919

Ross Youngs

Long before there was a Pete Rose there was a Ross Youngs. Youngs, playing for John McGraw from 1917 to 1926, set the style for nonstop hustle. Indeed, his nickname was "Pep."

A fine all-around athlete, the left-handed-batting Youngs teed off on big-league pitching from the first moment he saw it, hitting above .300 the first 7 years of his aborted career, including .351 in 1920 and .356 in 1924. A strong-armed outfielder, he led or tied for the lead 3 times in assists. He was one of the key men in the Giants' drive to 4 consecutive pennants in the early 1920s and was one of McGraw's personal favorites.

In 1925 Youngs's batting average slipped to .264. McGraw felt there was something wrong with his brilliant right-fielder, although Ross, with that sense of indestructibility peculiar to great athletes, laughed it off. In the spring of 1926, however, McGraw insisted Youngs submit to a medical examination. The 29-year-old ballplayer was found to be suffering from Bright's disease, a serious kidney disorder. Youngs managed to play 95 games in 1926 and bat .306. Finally too ill to continue, he left the team before the season ended. He spent most of the next year bedridden and died on October 22, 1927, at the age of 30, 2 years after the death of McGraw's other favorite ballplayer, Christy Mathewson. For years theirs were the only pictures that hung on the walls of John McGraw's Polo Grounds office.

Johnny Bench

For years it was heresy to mention the name of another catcher in the same breath as Bill Dickey and Mickey Cochrane. Not even Roy Campanella or Yogi Berra, it seemed, rated that high. Johnny Bench, however, may finally compel a revision of the greatest all-time team; barring that, he is the probable catcher on the second 50-year team that will be selected in the year 1999, with Dickey and Cochrane still battling it out for the number 1 spot on the 1900–1950 team.

By the time the 20-year-old Bench was in his second year, 1968, he was already hailed as destined for greatness. Early in Bench's career Ted Williams autographed a ball to him as follows: "To Johnny Bench, a sure Hall of Famer."

By his third full year, 1970, Bench was on his way to making a prophet of Williams. The young Cincinnati catcher hit 45 home runs, drove in 148 runs—leading the league in both departments—and was the National League's Most Valuable Player, an award he won again 2 years later when he hit 40 home runs and drove in 125 runs, again leading in each category. In 1974 he won still another RBI title, with 129.

A superlative defensive catcher, possessor of a most formidable throwing arm, a shrewd handler of pitchers, Bench has won as much admiration for his defensive skills as for his hitting. Indeed, if anything his catching has always been underrated, for his natural talents are so great that he has always made hard plays look easy and impossible plays look routine.

Ted Williams

Ted Williams was the greatest hitter of his time, and according to witnesses as far-ranging as Tris Speaker and Jimmy Dykes, the greatest of all time. For fans, and particularly for other ballplayers, there was a mystique about Williams that went beyond the purity of his swing and the explosive power it generated, beyond the fact that his .406 batting average in 1941 made him the last .400 hitter (it remains the highest single-season figure since Hornsby's .424 in 1924). Perhaps it was the passion of his commitment, the intensity of his concentration, his pursuit of perfection in the art of hitting. To some people, Ted Williams studying hitting was like William Shakespeare taking a creative-writing course. But Williams never lost his fascination for analyzing the art of smashing a well-thrown baseball with a bat.

He was an individualist, temperamental and uncompromising, and could be rude or charming, depending on his mood. He was, and is, admired and respected and even revered by the men whom he played with and against.

His acquisition by the Red Sox was fortuitous, with a storybook quality to it. In 1936, Red Sox General Manager Eddie Collins was on a scouting trip to the West Coast to look at a young second baseman, Bobby Doerr, who was playing with the San Diego club of the Pacific Coast League. Collins liked Doerr and bought his contract; but he also liked, to put it mildly, the tall skinny outfielder with the whiplash swing, and bought his contract, too. Eddie Collins had made the greatest discovery in California since John Marshall stumbled on gold at Sutter's Mill nearly a hundred years before.

Williams batted .327 in his rookie year with the Red Sox, in 1939. He wouldn't hit that low again until 1950. He led the league with 145 runs batted in. The 21-year-old slugger astonished both the opposition and the home-plate umpires with his uncanny knowledge of the strike zone, refusing to swing at pitches that were an inch—or even less—outside of it. His eyesight was phenomenal. He claimed he could follow the ball into home plate from the moment it left the pitcher's hand. (The

fact that he avoided beanballs with a flick of his head rather than flopping into the dirt bore out his claim.)

He batted .344 in 1940, and in 1941 had what must be described as an historic year. Williams proved many things on the last day of the 1941 season. He went into a doubleheader against the Athletics batting .3995, which worked out to a flat .400. Offered the chance to sit out the game by Red Sox manager Joe Cronin, Williams refused. If he was going to hit .400, he said, he would do it honestly.

He did it, and spectacularly. Playing both ends of the doubleheader, he connected for 6 hits in 8 at bats and ended the season with a .406 batting average. It was an exhibition of talent, guts, and self-confidence seldom seen in any sports arena.

He took another batting title the next year, hitting .356, and then entered the air force for 3 years. He returned in 1946, as lethal as ever. He won batting titles in 1947 and 1948 with averages of .343 and .369.

He was called up again during the Korean War and missed virtually all of the 1951–1952 seasons. What his record would look like if he had not lost nearly 5 prime years to the military is something baseball fans love to conjecture. He surely would have had at least another 200 home runs to go with his 521, and probably another 2 or 3 batting titles to go with the 6 he did win.

In 1957, the 39-year-old Williams astonished the baseball world by posting a monumental .388 batting average, and then the next year took his sixth and last batting title with a .328 average, at 40 years of age the oldest batting champion in history. In his final season, 1960, the 42-year-old Splendid

Splinter batted .316. His lifetime average is .344, topped in this century only by Ty Cobb, Rogers Hornsby, Shoeless Joe Jackson, and Tris Speaker among players in 1,000 or more games.

He led in home runs 4 times, runs batted in 4 times (159 in 1949, his high), runs scored 6 times, total bases 6 times, and slugging average 9 times. He won the Triple Crown in 1942 and 1947. He was voted the league's Most Valuable Player in 1946 and 1949, and failed to win that honor on some other occasions because some of the sports writers (who do the voting) didn't care for his personality.

Ted Williams in 1940

Power versus power:
Bob Feller pitching to Ted Williams.

Joe Medwick in 1936

Joe Medwick

They called him "Ducky," which he hated, because he walked with a slight waddle; and they also called him "Muscles," which meant they did not call him Ducky to his face. They also called him the best right-handed hitter in the National League in the 1930s. He hit above .300 his first 10 years in the league, with his .374 in 1937 part of a Triple Crown (the National League's last Triple Crown winner). In that season he led in batting, home runs, runs batted in, doubles, hits, runs scored, total bases, and slugging average.

A notorious "bad ball" hitter, swinging at pitches far out of the strike zone, the aggressive St. Louis Cardinal outfielder set a league record in 1936 with 64 doubles and tied another with 3 straight RBI titles (1936–1938).

He was a tough, moody character who played hard. His rough slide into Detroit third baseman Marv Owen in the seventh game of the 1934 World Series precipitated a riot and compelled Judge Landis to eject Joe from the game to prevent things from getting worse.

In 1940 the Cardinals sold him to Brooklyn, and a week later Joe suffered a horrifying beaning at the hands of Cardinal pitcher Bob Bowman, which may or may not have been deliberate. Joe recovered but was never again the fearsome hitter he had been, continuing to hit .300, but a less ferocious .300.

Medwick has a .324 lifetime batting average for a career that went from the early 1930s to the late 1940s.

Joe Medwick sliding into Detroit third baseman Marv Owen in the seventh game of the 1934 World Series in Detroit. This play precipitated a riot and led to Medwick's ejection.

Juan Marichal in 1965

Juan Marichal

Juan Marichal joined the Giants during their first year in San Francisco, 1958, thus depriving New York Giant fans of watching the finest Giant right-hander since Mathewson. The Dominican-born pitcher was quite an eyeful, too, with his picturesque high kick just before he delivered the ball.

Marichal's best seasons have a classic look on the printed page: 25–8 (1963), 21–8 (1964), 22–13 (1965), 25–6 (1966), 26–9 (1968), 21–11 (1969). His earned-run averages were consistently low, but only once did he lead the league (2.10 in 1969). And although his strikeouts went above 200 6 times, not even his 240 led in 1965. And therein lay Juan Marichal's problem: it was named Sandy Koufax, who was working at the same trade several hundred miles down the coast. Many of Juan's greatest years coincided with Sandy's even greater ones, and thus Marichal was overshadowed by his peerless contemporary (he never won a Cy Young Award, for instance, despite 3 years with 25 or more wins).

Nevertheless, Marichal, who had exceptional control for a power pitcher (36 walks in 307 innings in 1966), has one of the best pitching records in National League history. His lifetime winning percentage of .631, based on a won-lost record of 243–142, is topped only by Christy Mathewson, Grover Cleveland Alexander, Three-Fingered Brown, and Tom Seaver among twentieth-century pitchers with 200 or more victories. And his lifetime earned-run average of 2.89 is bettered in the league only by Seaver among pitchers with 3,000 or more innings pitched since 1920.

Nap Lajoie in 1908

Napoleon Lajoie

Napoleon "Nap" Lajoie, also known as "Larry" among his contemporaries, was the first "greatest second baseman of all time," predecessor to Eddie Collins and then Rogers Hornsby (who will probably hold the distinction until another second baseman matches his .358 lifetime batting average).

Lajoie, who played in the big leagues from 1896 to 1917 and batted .339 lifetime, was remembered by his contemporaries as being extraordinarily graceful in the field and for hitting bone-breaking line drives. He was the American League's big hitter in the days before Ty Cobb. In 1901, the first year the league was in business, Nap batted .422, which is still the league record. He also led the next 3 years, with batting averages of .378, .355, and .377. He was so dominant that when he was player-manager for Cleveland from 1905 to 1909 the team was known as the "Naps."

Lajoie's .422 is interesting for more reasons than one. For nearly a half century his average was posted as .405, but then closer study of the records revealed he actually had 10 or so more hits than had been recorded. This tells us not only how casual record keeping was in the good old days, but also something about Lajoie's lack of interest in his own heroics. Can you imagine a player today not knowing he had been short-changed in the hit column?

But of course Nap collected 3,251 safe ones in his career, and that's an awful lot of hits to chart.

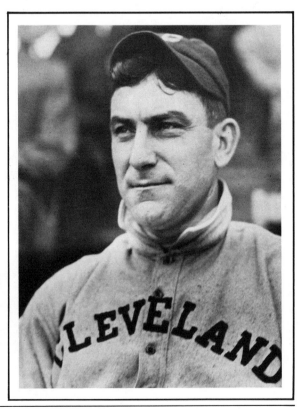

Joe DiMaggio in 1947

Joe DiMaggio

As efficient on the field as any player who ever lived, Joe DiMaggio never gave the impression that he was working very hard. A flawless piece of sculpture at the plate, feet spread wide, bat cocked high and still, he strode no more than a few inches as he moved to hit a ball as hard as it could be hit. Possessed of unerring judgment in center field, he always seemed to be waiting for the ball's descent, galloping under it with the graceful strides of a thoroughbred. He threw with apparent ease, but his pegs came in with sharpshooter velocity and accuracy. He was perhaps the most splendidly designed ball-playing machine ever to cast a shadow on a ball field.

Some cynic once asked Yankee manager Joe McCarthy if his perfect player could bunt. "I don't know," McCarthy answered, "and I have no intention of ever finding out."

A quiet man, shy with strangers, Joe DiMaggio possesses a magical name second only to Babe Ruth's in baseball lore. A full generation after his retirement, he remains the most avidly awaited guest at Old-Timers' Day ceremonies, cheered by fans who never saw him play. Reserved and undemonstrative, he nevertheless had a dynamic that his teammates regarded as inspirational. By performance alone, he commanded and he dominated.

The eighth of 9 children born to immigrant parents in Martinez, California, in 1914, Joe joined the San Francisco Seals of the Pacific Coast League in 1932. The next year, at the age of 18, he put together a 61-game hitting streak. The Seals' dream of selling him to a major-league club for a huge price was jolted the next season, however, when he injured his knee getting out of a taxi cab. Concern about the injury caused most clubs to shy away from investing in the youngster. The Yankees, however, were willing to take the gamble, and for $25,000 and 5 minor-league players bought Joe's contract.

In his rookie year, 1936, Joe made the gamble into a bargain—he hit .323 (2 points under what would ultimately be his lifetime batting average) and drove in 125 runs. A year later he batted .346, drove in 167 runs, and hit a league-leading 46 home runs, an incredible number for a right-handed hitter in Yankee Stadium. He kept getting better. In 1939 he led the league with a .381 batting average, then led again in 1940 with a .352 mark. He batted .357 in 1941, but that was the year Ted Williams hit .406. Nevertheless, it was DiMaggio who dominated baseball in 1941.

On May 15, 1941, DiMaggio got a single in 4 at bats against the White Sox. That 1-bagger was the first trickle of a current that was to pour forward through 2 months and 56 games and make baseball history. The 56-game hitting streak is the most sustained 1-man drama in all sports. Game after game the streak mounted to more and more heroic proportions. Through a building pressure which was to be matched only by Roger Maris's quest for Ruth's home-run record in 1961, the nerveless DiMaggio kept hitting. On June 29 he hit in both games of a doubleheader against Washington, breaking George Sisler's American League record of 41 straight games. A few days later he broke Willie Keeler's pre-1900 record of 44. He was getting hotter, too. Over the streak's final 10 games he went 23 for 40, an average of .575, under the most excruciating pressure. The end finally came on the night of July 17, in

Joe DiMaggio, traveling by train during the 1938 season

Cleveland. Ken Keltner's 2 excellent stops at third base helped spell finis to this marvelous record. (Joe went on to hit in his next 17 games before being stopped again.)

An overlooked statistic of Joe's in that unforgettable 1941 season is the fact that he went to the plate 541 times and, although a hard swinger, struck out just 13 times.

DiMaggio entered the army for 3 years after the 1942 season. His greatest postwar year was 1948, when he batted .320 and led the league with 39 home runs and 155 runs batted in, playing most of the time in great pain because of a bone spur on his right heel. A postseason operation supposedly removed the problem, but Joe suffered a recurrence the following spring. The 1949 season opened with DiMaggio on the sidelines, his return to the lineup problematic.

It was not until the end of June that DiMaggio was able to get back into action, setting the stage for a comeback no fiction writer would have dared concoct.

The Yankees were opening a 3-game series at Fenway Park against the Red Sox, with whom they would fight down to the last day of the season before winning the pennant. Coming back cold, with nothing more than batting practice, DiMaggio put on a 1-man 3-game show that devastated the Sox. He won the first game with a 2-run homer, hit 2 more home runs to win the game the next night, and then won the third game with still another home run. He drove in 9 runs in the 3 games. Once in the lineup, he stayed there, playing in 76 games, batting .346 and knocking in 67 runs.

After batting .263 in 1951, DiMaggio, then approaching 37, retired. He might have hung on for another couple of seasons, but a man who was motivated in large part by pride would never allow himself to be less than perfect on a ball field. Joe DiMaggio was not only a player who set records; he was also a man who set standards.

DiMaggio among his peers: with Mantle and Williams (above); *with Gehrig* (below)

Joe DiMaggio hitting a home run off the Giants' Sal Maglie in the fourth game of the 1951 World Series at the Polo Grounds. It was the last home run Joe ever hit.

Steve Carlton in 1967

Steve Carlton

After the 1971 season, in which he was 20–9 for the Cardinals, Steve Carlton got into a salary dispute with his employers. The Cardinals owner, Gussie Busch, a hard-headed gentleman, decided to trade his star lefty rather than yield to Carlton's demands. So Steve went to the Phillies for right-hander Rick Wise. St. Louis had made a mistake, trading a great pitcher for a good one.

The dimensions of the mistake became apparent the next year when Carlton tore up the league. Pitching for a last-place team, he won 27 and lost 10, posted a 1.97 earned-run average, struck out 310 batters, and pitched 8 shutouts. He was a runaway Cy Young Award winner (he won again in 1977 and 1980) and was one of the biggest drawing cards in Philadelphia history that summer.

He won 46 percent of his team's victories.

Carlton has gone on and on. He has so far won 249 games, including 20–7 and 23–10 seasons in 1976 and 1977 and 24–9 in 1980.

His greatest game, on the night of September 15, 1969, was, ironically, a losing effort. On that night he fanned 19 New York Mets, only to lose 4–3 on a pair of 2-run home runs by Mets outfielder Ron Swoboda. The 19 strikeouts are a 1-game record, a record Carlton shares with Tom Seaver and Nolan Ryan.

Possessor of a live fastball and what has been described as the game's most devastating slider, Carlton has become the National League's finest left-hander since Sandy Koufax.

Brooks Robinson in 1966

Brooks Robinson

Aladdin had his lamp, Merlin had his wand, and Brooks Robinson had his glove, and what magic the 3 did weave.

Early in his career with the Baltimore Orioles, Robinson went into a hitting slump and his manager, Paul Richards, decided to sit him down for a while. But the pitchers wouldn't hear of it. "They wanted him in there," Richards said. "They didn't care if he never got a hit." Brooks was "in there" for 23 years, from 1955 to 1977, all of it in an Orioles uniform, a longevity record for a player with a single club.

Robinson owns the highest lifetime fielding average for a third baseman in 1,000 or more games (.971). His 2,870 games at third is another record. Most lifetime assists, putouts, chances, double plays—the records belong to Brooks Robinson. He led American League third basemen 11 times in fielding, and 8 times in assists.

The modest, low-keyed, likable Robinson could hit, too. In 1964 he batted .317, led in runs batted in with 118, and was voted the league's Most Valuable Player. He hit more than 20 home runs 6 times. He dominated the 1970 World Series with a .429 batting average as well as with his phenomenal fielding at third base. Brooks completed his career with 2,848 hits.

Going to his left, backhanding shots down the line, and, most spectacularly of all, coming in for bunts and slow rollers and throwing runners out with a swooping pickup and toss, Brooks Robinson set the modern standard for how third base should be played.

Brooks Robinson makes a routine play at third base.

Jim Rice

Jim Rice of the Boston Red Sox was the American League's premier hitter for the last half of the 1970s. Averaging out the 5-year period from 1975 (his first full season) through 1979, Rice led American League hitters in home runs, hits, total bases, slugging, runs batted in, runs scored, and extra base hits. He was second in triples, and—unusual for a power hitter in today's game—tied for third in batting average.

Leading the league in total bases for 3 consecutive years (1977–1979), Rice tied a league record set by Ty Cobb in 1907–1909. His 406 total bases in 1978 were the highest since DiMaggio's 418 in 1937. It was a golden year for Rice, as he also led in home runs (46), triples (15), hits (213), runs batted in (139), and slugging average (.600). Leading in

both home runs and triples is a most unusual feat. Before Rice, only Mickey Mantle and Sam Crawford had done it in the American League. Jim could have been declared the league's Most Valuable Player the day the 1978 season ended, but instead the sports writers waited for the formality of the vote a few months later.

Rice also took the home-run crown in 1977 with 39, and the slugging title that year with .593.

Jim Rice, the Boston Strong Man, will cause a lot of head-scratching when it comes time to select the all-time Red Sox outfield. Assuming there are 5 outstanding candidates—Ted Williams, Tris Speaker, Carl Yastrzemski, Fred Lynn, and Jim Rice—which 3 would you choose?

Shoeless Joe Jackson in 1911; his fancy footwear belies his nickname.

"Shoeless" Joe Jackson

They called him "Shoeless" Joe and his is one of the saddest stories in sports. His full name was Joseph Jefferson Jackson. He was born in a South Carolina mill town in 1888 and as a youngster supposedly played baseball without wearing shoes. He was illiterate. When he was in the big leagues and went out to dinner with some of his teammates he would order last, after hearing what was written on a menu that he could not read.

He was a fearsome hitter. When baseball men whose experience covered large tracts of time were asked who was the purest, most natural hitter they ever saw, they invariably answered Ted Williams or Joe Jackson. Ernie Shore, who pitched for the Red Sox in the 1910s, tells about Joe. "He just hit everything you threw up there. And I mean he *hit* it. There's a difference between getting your bat on the ball and hitting it, if you know what I mean. He once lined a ball between my legs that didn't touch the ground until it got out behind second base. . . . There was no way you could fool him with a pitch. Every time he put his bat on the ball it was a line drive."

Jackson first came to the big leagues with the Philadelphia Athletics for a few games in 1908 and 1909, but somehow did not impress the normally sharp-eyed Connie Mack. The outfielder came back in 1911 with Cleveland and in his first full year batted .408. In American League history only 4 averages have been higher—but one of them was Cobb's .420 the same year. Jackson batted .395 the next year, but again Cobb would not be denied, hitting .410. In 1914 Joe batted .373 but still did not lead; Cobb wouldn't hear of it. Ty hit .390. Leave it to the joyless Cobb to take the fun out of batting .408, .395, and .373.

Jackson was traded to the White Sox in 1915, helped them to a pennant in 1917 and another in 1919. The 1919 White Sox were a very strong team; they were also a woefully underpaid team. Most ballplayers were underpaid in those years and there was a lot of betting on games by players, and probably more games were fixed than we will ever know.

The Sox were top-heavy favorites to win

the 1919 World Series over the Cincinnati Reds. But they lost, and the odor was strong. The odor continued to be strong into the 1920 season. The White Sox were apparently on the way to another pennant, good enough to win when they wanted to, unsavory enough to throw a game when the price was right.

Joe Jackson in 1917

The scandal finally broke in late September 1920: 8 White Sox players were suspended. Jackson, hitting .382, was among them. They were accused of throwing the 1919 Series to Cincinnati and were barred forever from organized baseball by Judge Landis.

Much of the story behind the scandal of the 1919 Series remains clouded, confused by differing versions, particularly Jackson's participation. Joe at one point confessed to a grand jury that he had been part of the monkey business, but the confession was stolen from the grand jury files and Joe later recanted. He and his 7 teammates were found innocent in a civil court, but Landis had already decided to give them the boot. The judge was an unforgiving man and never entertained an appeal on Joe's behalf.

Finished at the age of 32 and with a bat still full of scorchers, Jackson returned to South Carolina where, it is nice to report, the homefolk never shunned him but rather regarded him as a hero to the end of his days, more sinned against than sinning.

He died in 1951, proprietor of a liquor store and owner of a lifetime batting average of .356—the third highest in baseball history—and barred from the Hall of Fame. Whatever Joe did or did not do, it's a long time past now, time for a game which denied Blacks entrance until 1946 to end its pose of total purity. The Hall of Fame should induct Joe Jackson, shoes and all.

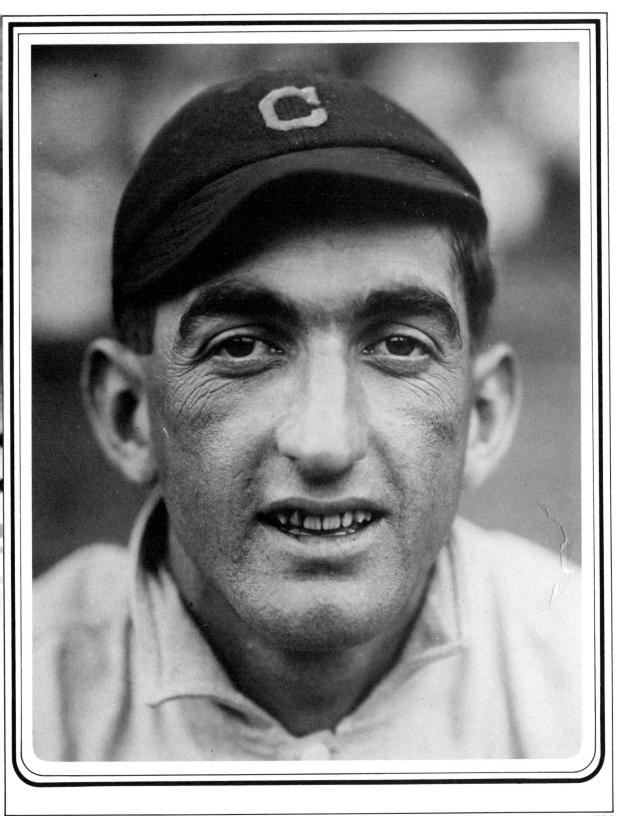

Frank Robinson

Frank Robinson was a bomber from Day One. Coming to the big leagues with the Cincinnati Reds in 1956, the 21-year-old right-handed-hitting outfielder tied Wally Berger's record for a rookie with 38 home runs. It was a debut at once auspicious and prophetic, as Robinson went on to become one of the game's hardest hitters through a career that lasted 21 years, from 1956 to 1976.

In 1961 he was voted the National League's Most Valuable Player, with 37 home runs, 124 runs batted in, and a league-leading slugging mark of .611, one of 3 consecutive slugging titles he took in 1960–1962.

He was perhaps the greatest hitter in Cincinnati history, but in 1965 the 30-year-old Robinson was traded to Baltimore, the logic being that Frank was "an old 30." Whoever made this physiological diagnosis was all wet. Robinson went to work in 1966 with Baltimore with a vengeance, winning the Triple Crown with a .316 batting average, 49 home runs, and 122 runs batted in, and became the only man ever to win Most Valuable Player awards in both leagues.

Robinson ended his career with 586 home runs, fourth on the all-time list, and 2,943 hits. He never seemed interested in those last 57 hits.

A man of fine leadership qualities, Robinson became baseball's first Black manager when he took over the reins of the Cleveland Indians in 1975.

The heart of the Baltimore Orioles' attack in the late 1960s. **Left to right:** *John "Boog" Powell, Brooks Robinson, Frank Robinson (plus an extra hand from backstage)*

The Philadelphia Phillies' Gavvy Cravath (left) and Tris Speaker doing the traditional thing before the 1915 World Series

Tris Speaker

Part of the catechism baseball fans learn at an early age is that the all-time greatest outfield is Babe Ruth, Ty Cobb, and Tris Speaker. Although certain revisionists may rebel and replace Speaker with DiMaggio, Tris seems a sound choice as the game's most indelible center fielder. He played an extremely shallow center field—which could be done in those days of the dead ball—so shallow that he made 4 unassisted double plays in his career. His great speed and ability to go back prevented balls from being hit over his head. He had a powerful throwing arm, leading the league in assists in 4 of his first 6 full years.

One of Speaker's problems was that his career was almost exactly contemporaneous with Cobb's (Tris played from 1907 to 1928). Whatever Tris did at the plate, Ty did a little better, except in 1916 when Speaker won the batting title with .386—the only time between 1907 and 1919 that Cobb did not win it. Speaker's lifetime batting average is a robust .344. He hit over .370 6 times, drove out 3,515 hits, and is the all-time specialist in doubles, hitting a grand total of 793 and leading the league 8 times.

Speaker began his career with the Red Sox and was traded to Cleveland just before the 1916 season opened. The problem was money. Tris wanted $15,000, the Sox were offering $9,000. The deal broke the hearts of Red Sox fans. But it was just a warm-up—a few years later the Red Sox traded away Babe Ruth.

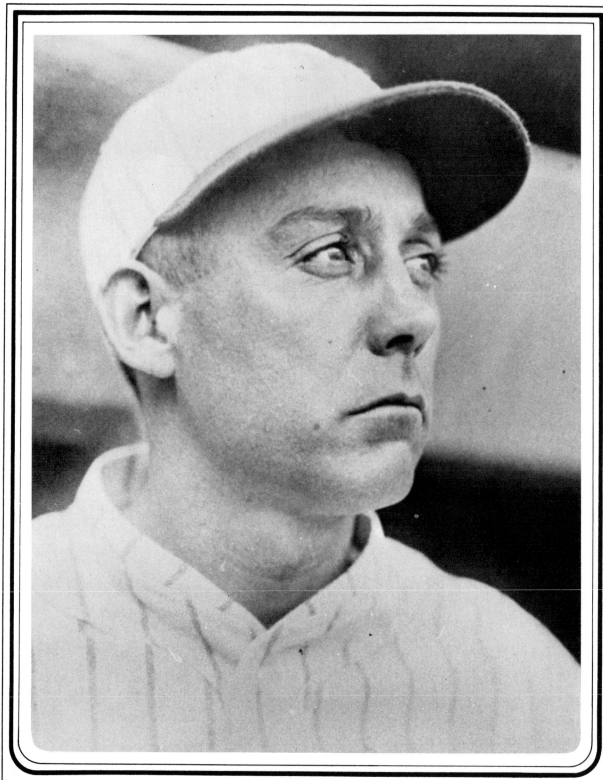

Edd Roush in 1922

Edd Roush

John McGraw was an autocrat. He would not tolerate backtalk from his players. Unfortunately for John J., two of his best in the 1920s were Frank Frisch and Bill Terry, who refused to take any nonsense. But before Frisch and Terry there was Edd Roush.

Roush, a superbly gifted center fielder—defensively, he was called the Tris Speaker of the National League—joined the Giants in 1916 and made it clear he did not care for McGraw. The Giants manager made a mistake and traded Edd to Cincinnati, where Roush flourished. In 1917 he led the league in batting with a .341 average, then led again in 1919 with .321. As far as consistency is concerned, Roush's batting averages from 1917 through 1926 read: .341, .333, .321, .339, .352, .352, .351, .348, .339, and .323.

Much to his dismay, Roush was reacquired by the Giants in 1927. A man who knew his own value, he squeezed a lucrative 3-year contract out of McGraw, who had never ceased regretting trading him. When the contract ran out after the 1929 season, it was renewed for less money than Roush thought he deserved. He held out. Being a man of character and high principle, when Edd Roush held out, he held out—he sat out the

entire 1930 season, the last player of stature to hold still for principle (not to mention money) for a full year.

McGraw traded him back to the Reds in 1931, Roush's last year in the big leagues.

Honus Wagner in 1906

Honus Wagner

That most gaudy accolade of all—"The Greatest Player Who Ever Lived"—is given most sparingly. It has, in fact, been seriously applied to only 3 players: Ty Cobb, Babe Ruth, and Honus Wagner. McGraw, with perhaps a dollop of National League prejudice, called Wagner the greatest of all players. So did many others. He remains legendary, as do Ruth and Cobb and Walter Johnson and very few others. He is to shortstops what Shakespeare is to playwrights. He dominates the position like a colossus.

He was a sweet-natured man, growing into a beloved foxy grandpa who was a teller of tall tales. In his prime he had the upper torso of a fullback and notoriously bowed legs. His hands were enormous. Among the many legends that have accrued to him is the one that has him picking up handfuls of dirt and pebbles along with the ball and firing the lot to first base. He made a large number of errors, but so did most infielders in those days of ragtag gloves and uneven infields.

Along with his scoop-shovel hands, he was blessed with remarkable running speed for a

Honus Wagner being properly rewarded

Honus Wagner safe at home at the Polo Grounds, about 1910

big man, stealing a total of 722 bases and leading the league 5 times.

He was a powerful hitter for a shortstop—indeed, for anybody. He holds the National League record for batting titles with 8, winning them in 1900, 1903, 1904, 1906, 1907, 1908, 1909, and 1911. Although he did not post the monumental batting averages of Ty Cobb or Joe Jackson, he did hit .381 in 1900 and .363 in 1905 (a year he did not win the title). He batted over .300 for 17 consecutive years, a National League record. His 252 triples are also a league record, while his 651 doubles place him second to Stan Musial in the National League.

Through the years in a career that ex-tended from 1897 to 1917, Wagner led the National League 7 times in doubles, 3 times in triples, 5 times in runs battle in, and 6 times in slugging, in addition to his 8 batting crowns.

The combination of affable, easygoing unpretentiousness with stunning athletics made him a folk hero in his time. He abhorred cigarettes. Once, when a tobacco manufacturer put Wagner's likeness on cards that were sold with packs of cigarettes, Honus threatened legal action. The card was withdrawn; the few that were printed command thousands of dollars in the collector's market today. Incredibly, Honus had little interest in money. In 1908 he signed a contract for

The all-time greatest shortstop

$10,000 a year and until the end of his career kept earning the same amount, never asking for a raise. When Pittsburgh owner Barney Dreyfuss asked him each year what he wanted, Wagner would reply, "Same as last year."

Among his tall tales was the time he was going for a ground ball and instead picked up and threw a rabbit that was just then crossing the infield. "I got the runner by a hare," said Honus. Another time, he claimed, he came up to pinch hit in the bottom of the ninth with the score tied. "I hit the ball over the fence," he said, "and was so excited I ran the bases the wrong way, starting up the third-base line. When I came around and touched home plate they subtracted a run and we lost."

A few years ago an interviewer asked Burleigh Grimes who was the greatest short-stop he ever saw. "Wagner," the old pitcher said. When it was pointed out that Grimes, who played from 1916 through 1934, saw Wagner at the end of the line, when Honus was well along in years, Grimes said, "I don't care how old he was. Wagner is the greatest shortstop I ever saw."

It seems 3 things are destined for perma-nence in this ever-changing world: death, taxes, and Wagner as all-time shortstop.

Dodger first baseman Steve Garvey has just homered in the National League Championship Series against Pittsburgh on October 9, 1974. The enthusiastic gentleman behind him is coach and future manager Tom LaSorda.

Steve Garvey

Going into the 1981 season, Los Angeles Dodgers first baseman Steve Garvey had played in 835 consecutive games. Only 5 men have ever shown more durability, and with another two seasons of uninterrupted work Garvey could pass 3 of them.

Garvey is out there every day because he can do 2 things—hit and field, requirements sufficient unto the job. For 3 years running (1975–1977) he led National League first basemen on defense, his .998 fielding average in 1976 establishing a league record for first basemen playing more than 150 games.

First basemen, however, are paid primarily to hit, and this Garvey has done with superb consistency. Since becoming a regular in 1973, he has hit over .300 in 7 of 8 seasons, dipping to .297 in 1977, the only year since 1974 he failed to collect 200 or more hits. With batting averages of .312, .319, and .317 in 1974–1976 and .316 and .315 in 1978–1979, Garvey seems mired in a rut of excellence. He has driven in more than 100 runs 5 times. In 1974 he was voted the National League's Most Valuable Player.

Garvey, whose image of politeness, courtesy, and consideration for others seems to have upset some of his teammates from time to time (he had an uncharacteristic and highly publicized clubhouse brawl with Don Sutton in 1978), is one of the game's top pressure players. In 3 Championship Series he had a batting average of .367 and for 3 World Series, .319.

Zack Wheat in 1915

"Zack" Wheat

Zachariah "Zack" Wheat joined the Brooklyn Dodgers in 1909 and remained for 18 years, a fixture in left field. He became during his tenure probably the most popular man ever to play in Brooklyn. Zack earned this admiration by his quiet, gentlemanly comportment, and also for the way he bashed line drives in all directions.

Wheat, for whom the Dodgers paid the Mobile club of the Southern League the modest sum of $1,200, was pretty much all they had to cheer about in Brooklyn for a lot of long, lean years. But Zack, whom his teammates called Buck, did give his fans their money's worth. He was a fine outfielder and a steady, solid hitter. In his 18 years in Brooklyn, he batted over .300 13 times, leading the league with a .338 average in 1918. Not a home-run hitter, even though he played into the days of the lively ball, Wheat racked up enough hits (2,884) to earn a lifetime .317 average.

Zack saved his best for his last years in Brooklyn. In 1923, at the age of 35, he batted .375. It felt so good that he batted .375 again the following year, banging out 212 hits. A year later, then 37 years old, he batted .359, with 221 hits. Coming as they did in the midst of Hornsby's .400 devastation, none of Wheat's averages were good enough to lead the league. But they made Brooklyn proud.

Wheat played his last year for the Philadelphia Athletics in 1927 and went out a .324 hitter.

Gabby Hartnett in 1927

"Gabby" Hartnett

The date was September 28, 1938. The Cubs were playing the Pirates at Wrigley Field. It was a head-to-head match for the National League pennant, with the Pirates holding a half-game lead. It was the bottom of the ninth, there were 2 out, the bases were empty, the score was tied, and the Cubs' player-manager Charles Leo "Gabby" Hartnett was up. With darkness already fallen, he would be the game's last batter. Pirate reliever Mace Brown grooved one and Hartnett, swinging where he judged the ball to be (it was that dark), met it squarely and drove it into the left-field bleachers. The home run, one of the most famous in baseball history—the celebrated "homer in the gloaming"—broke the spirit of the Pirates and the Cubs went on to win the pennant.

Hartnett, who caught from 1922 to 1941, all but the last year with the Cubs, was the great home-run hitter among catchers until the coming of Roy Campanella and Yogi Berra. Gabby hit 236 long ones, with a high of 37 in 1930, a year when he batted .339. In 1935 he batted .344 and 2 years later .354, 4 points under Chief Meyers's National League record for catchers.

Gabby was a premium defensive catcher, leading in fielding 6 times and assists 6 times. His arm was so powerful that fans would come out early to watch infield practice, just to see Hartnett fire line drives around the bases. There are those who believe Gabby possessed the strongest throwing arm of any catcher in history.

Mickey Mantle

If Mickey Mantle had played 50 or 60 years ago, we would be hearing tall tales today from the old-timers about the kid outfielder the Yankees had who could hit a ball left-handed as far as Ruth and right-handed as far as Foxx, who could outrun anybody in the league, and who had an arm like a cannon.

None of it sounds very plausible, and the truth is the kid did not do it 50 or 60 years ago; he did it in the 1950s and 1960s. A lot of people saw it in person and a lot more on television when he almost became the first man to hit a fair ball out of Yankee Stadium (that was batting left-handed), and when he hit a clout in Washington (right-handed) that was measured by rational people out to 565 feet. He smashed home runs right- and left-handed in the same game 10 times, a record that still stands.

He was one of the most total concentrations of pure, unadulterated baseball-playing talent of all time. He was an Oklahoma boy, a hayseed in the finest American tradition, when Yankee scout Tom Greenwade signed

him for something like a $1,000 bonus. Named after his father's favorite player, Mickey Cochrane, Mantle was one of the toughest and most dynamic players ever. Plagued by injuries throughout his career, he played through the pain without complaint. His record is impressive as it stands; what it might have looked like had Mantle been

Mickey Mantle, Yankee rookie, in 1951

injury-free is another reverie for the romantics to indulge.

He played for 18 years, from 1951 to 1968, and like Willie Mays, who came to the big leagues the same year as Mantle, he hung on for a few years too many. His greatest season was 1956, when he became the sixth Triple Crown winner in American League history, on the strength of a .353 batting average, 52 home runs, and 130 runs batted in. He hit .365 the next year but ran flush into Ted Williams's .388. In 1961 he hit 54 home runs, finishing second to teammate Roger Maris's record-smashing 61. (One great advantage Maris had in that memorable season was Mantle batting behind him.)

The league's Most Valuable Player in 1956, 1957, and 1962, Mantle led 4 times in home runs, once in triples, 6 times in runs scored, and 4 times in slugging average. His awesome power from either side of the plate so intimidated opposing pitchers that he led the league 5 times in bases on balls, drawing more than 100 10 times, including his last year, when he batted a feeble .237.

Helping to hammer the Yankees into 12 World Series in his 18 seasons, Mantle holds numerous Series records, including 18 home runs, 40 runs batted in, and 42 runs scored. Lifetime, Mickey hit 536 home runs, placing him sixth on the all-time list.

Joe DiMaggio's last season was 1951, which was also Mickey Mantle's first. That is how you perpetuate a dynasty.

Cy Young in 1900

"Cy" Young

Until a ballplayer named Most Valuable comes along, Denton True "Cy" Young will remain the only man to have a major award named for him.

Although Young pitched the entire decade of the 1890s, he also pitched 11 years into the twentieth century, making him the only major star who was equally brilliant on both sides of the 1900 barrier.

Young's career is astonishing not just for its 22-year longevity, but also for its constant productivity. After winning more than 20 games 9 times from 1891 to 1899 (including totals of 36, 32, and 35), he went on to 7 more 20-plus seasons from 1900 to 1908, with years of 33–10, 32–10, and 28–9 in 1901, 1902, and 1903. Overall he won 511 games, undoubtedly the most secure pitching record in the books (as is his 313 losses; no pitcher will top

that unless one comes along whose father owns the team). Just as eye-blinking are his 753 complete games in 816 starts. Give that one some thought.

At the age of 41 in 1908, he still had enough to win 21 and lose 12 for the Red Sox, complete 30 of 33 starts, and put up a 1.26 earned-run average. In 299 innings he walked only 37.

Young, who pitched in an era when the ball was juiced up on the outside instead of inside, was apparently pretty quick. The "Cy" was short for his original nickname, "Cyclone," after his fastball. When he was in his 80s he told an interviewer he had been as fast as Walter Johnson and Bob Feller. An old man might embroider a bit, but the record book doesn't lie.

Carl Yastrzemski

In 1967, when Carl Yastrzemski won the Triple Crown and was voted the American League's Most Valuable Player, the Boston Red Sox left fielder showed just how good a ballplayer could be. Leading the Red Sox up from a ninth-place finish the year before, Yastrzemski batted .326, hit 44 home runs, and drove in 121 runs. Over the last 10 pressure-packed games, he batted above .500 and led the Red Sox to their first pennant in 21 years, a pennant they won on the last day of the season.

Yaz joined the Red Sox in 1961 as a highly touted bonus player. Accused by some of his managers of occasionally being lethargic in his play, particularly when the Red Sox team around him was an uninspiring one, he has a spotty page in the record book. Along with his Triple Crown, he won 2 other batting championships (in 1963 and 1968), led in doubles 3 times, hits twice, and slugging average 3 times. Yet in his 20 seasons he hit better than .300 only 6 times.

Nevertheless, his all-around talents are explosive, in the field as well as at bat. In 1977 his fielding was letter perfect—1.000 for 140 games in the outfield and 10 at first base. Owner of an arm that is half shotgun and half radar, he has led the league outfielders a record 7 times in assists. In 1979 he became the first American Leaguer to compile over 3,000 hits and 400 home runs.

Paul Waner

Paul Waner was not a large man—he stood just under 5 feet 9 inches tall and weighed around 150 pounds—and he had a most unorthodox style of hitting, resting the bat on his shoulder until the pitcher was about to deliver. But then he uncoiled with the sudden strength of a steel spring, whipping the bat with enormously powerful wrists and hitting bulletlike line drives. And he usually did hit the ball, too; in a career that stretched from 1926, when he came up with the Pirates, to 1945, embracing 2,549 games and 9,459 at bats, Paul Waner struck out only 376 times.

Paul and his younger brother Lloyd, who followed him into the Pittsburgh outfield in 1927 and played alongside him for 14 years, were born in the palindrome town of Harrah, Oklahoma. Brought up on a farm, the boys' penchant for baseball was abetted by their father, who played some semi-pro ball around Oklahoma when he could get away from his chores. Mostly it was Paul and Lloyd, pitching to each other. But it was not bats and balls they were using; those luxuries were not always readily available. So they broke corn cobs in half and fired those to one another, trying to hit them with sawed-down broom handles. Both brothers said later it was great practice because those corn cobs would break every which way. It taught them to follow a pitched ball and move their bats quickly.

Paul joined the Pirates in 1926 at the age of 23. The quiet, self-effacing rookie served notice immediately: he batted .336 and led the league with 22 triples. A year later he did even better. He won the first of his 3 batting titles with a .380 average, led again in triples with 17, in hits with 237, and in runs batted in with 131. The following year he hit .370, and then went on with averages of .336, .368, .322, .341, .309, .362 (in 1934, his second batting title), .321, .373 (in 1936, his third title), and .354. Finally in 1938 he slipped under .300 for the first time in 12 years.

In 1932 Waner set a league record with 62 doubles, only to see it broken by Joe Medwick's 64 in 1936. He collected more than 200 hits a season 8 times.

In 1942 Paul became only the sixth man

and second National Leaguer (after Honus Wagner) in this century to accumulate 3,000 hits (he finished up with a total of 3,152). His lifetime batting average is .333. Among twentieth-century National Leaguers with 1,000 games or more, Paul's average is topped only by Rogers Hornsby and Bill Terry.

Paul Waner

Waner was a sociable and highly intelligent man—one of his roommates remembers him reading Seneca "to pass the time"—and a whimsical one. "They say money talks," he once said. "But all it's ever said to me is 'Goodbye.'"

He was also, throughout much of his life, an alcoholic. If only half the stories are true, Waner was a prodigious drinker. He was sometimes an early morning drinker. When it neared time to leave for the ball park, his roommate said, the agile Waner would execute a dozen or so backflips until he was sober.

One day he reported to the ball park with a hangover, his head aching and his eyes bleary. He proceeded to line 4 hits. Later, he told someone that each time he came to the plate he was seeing 3 baseballs. "Then how the hell did you manage to get four hits?" he was asked. "I swung at the one in the middle," Waner replied.

It has been said that Waner's knowledge of the art of hitting was second only to Ted Williams's. However sophisticated his theories, Waner could at the same time be very basic. Noticing one day how finicky some of his Pittsburgh teammates were about their bat selection, he told the batboy to indiscriminately hand him a different bat each time he went to the plate. Waner went to the plate 5 times that afternoon and got 4 hits.

"It isn't the bat," Paul said after the game, "it's the man who's wheeling it." It helps immeasurably, of course, when the man is Paul Waner.

Lloyd Waner

Ted Lyons

"If he had pitched for the Yankees," Joe McCarthy once said of right-hander Ted Lyons, "he would have won four hundred games." McCarthy may have been right. Pitching from 1923 to 1946 for the White Sox, a team that played .500 ball only 7 times during Lyons's long tenure, he still managed to win 260 games and lose 230 for a .531 winning percentage.

Coming to the White Sox straight from the campus of Baylor University, the 23-year-old Lyons had a live fastball. He was a 20-game winner in 1925, 1927, and 1930. Then he hurt his arm and had to change his style of pitching. Throwing breaking stuff, changes, and knuckleballs, Ted was able to make a successful transition from a power pitcher to

a canny one. He kept pitching and kept winning, despite the mediocre teams he played for.

In 1942, the 42-year-old Lyons had an exceptionally fine year. He won 14 and lost 6 (for a sixth-place team), led the league in earned-run average with a 2.10 mark, and completed all 20 of his starts. (Pitching in the modern era, Lyons had a remarkable completion record—484 starts, 356 complete games.)

After the 1942 season Lyons enlisted in the marines and was away for 3 years. When he returned after the war he made a few starts, then retired early in the 1946 season to manage the team he had pitched for so gallantly for nearly a quarter of a century.

Wes Ferrell

Wes Ferrell was a pitcher and he was a hitter. He rates a place among the game's greatest for being one of the most potent double threats in its history.

Wes was tough, temperamental, colorful, likable, handsome, and a big winner. He joined the Cleveland Indians in 1929 and began throwing his high, rising fastball right by all and sundry. He set a record by winning 20 or more games in his first 4 big-league seasons, and overall was a 20-game winner 6 times, twice winning 25 (1930 and 1935). Wes was a workhorse, leading in games twice, complete games twice, and innings pitched 3 times.

After a sore arm deprived him of his fastball in 1933, he became a stuff pitcher, winning big for the Red Sox, to whom Cleveland traded him in 1934 and where he formed an outstanding battery with his catcher-brother Rick.

Temperamental, yes. He was known to grind his wristwatch under his heel and rip his glove apart after losing a close game. And handsome, too. Hollywood offered him a screen test in the 1930s, but Wes told them, "I already have a job."

He was one of the hardest-hitting pitchers in baseball history. In 1931 he set a season home-run record for pitchers that still stands—9—while batting .319. He also holds the lifetime home-run record for pitchers, 36 (he hit 2 others as a pinch-hitter). In 1935 he batted .347. His lifetime batting average is .280, while on the mound he won 193 and lost 128.

Johnny Mize in 1950

Johnny Mize

No one can offer a reasonable explanation why Johnny Mize is not in the Hall of Fame. Year after year the electors scandalously overlook the man who after Bill Terry is probably the National League's greatest first baseman. Mize was one of the most fearsome sluggers of all time.

Big John joined the Cardinals in 1936 and ripped off 9 .300-plus seasons in a row, including a .364 batting average in 1937 and a league-leading .349 2 years later. His lifetime batting average is .312 and he hit a total of 359 home runs (despite spending 3 prime seasons in the navy), while his lifetime slugging average of .562 is eighth highest in history and second only to Hornsby in the National League.

Mize led or tied for the lead in home runs 4 times, with a high of 51 in 1947. He took 4 slugging titles, 3 RBI titles, and also led once each in doubles and triples. He holds the major-league record for hitting 3 home runs in a game, having done it 6 times.

The Cardinals traded him to the Giants in 1942, and the Giants sent him to the Yankees in 1949, where he began a second career as a part-time player and murderous pinch-hitter, helping the Yankees to their 5 consecutive pennants and World Championships.

Cooperstown . . .

Infielder Jimmy Brown (left) *and Johnny Mize in 1937*

Harry Heilmann

And now let us examine the strange case of Harry Heilmann, stellar right-handed-hitting outfielder for Detroit in the 1920s. What mysterious elixir did he imbibe in 1921, 1923, 1925, and 1927? For it was in those odd-numbered years that Harry led the American League in hitting with such thunderous batting averages as .394, .403, .393, and .398. Harry was just 9 hits away from being a 4-time .400 hitter.

Some cynics have reported that Heilmann worked on 2-year contracts that expired in odd-numbered years, thus accounting for his biennial revivals. Maybe. But Harry wasn't exactly mashed potatoes in the even-numbered years, hitting .356, .346, and .367.

He joined the Tigers in 1914 but didn't have his first .300 season until 1919. Beginning in that year and through the 1930 season (when he was with Cincinnati), Heilmann averaged .357 for the decade. His batting average for 1921–1927, his heyday years, was .379. His lifetime mark isn't bad either—.342, seventh in this century for players with 1,000 games or more.

Harry was a line-drive hitter, specializing in doubles. He collected more than 40 of these half-a-homers 8 times, and 542 lifetime. He got more than 200 hits 4 times, and 8 times drove in more than 100 runs. He is one of the half-dozen greatest right-handed hitters, who ever smiled at a pitcher.

Walter Johnson

Walter Johnson was the fastest pitcher who ever lived. How do we know this? Because everybody says so. Who is "everybody"? Well, everybody who saw him pitch and almost everybody who didn't. There are certain clues, too. Talk to ballplayers of the past and you will hear those who say "I got my share off of Feller," or "Grove didn't make his living off of me," and so on. Some of this may be elderly gentlemen stretching a fact or two, though much of it may be true. But listen to them talk about Walter Johnson: "I never saw it." "You could actually *hear* it go past you." "I got a loud foul and counted myself damned lucky." Walter Johnson on the mound was something akin to Babe Ruth at bat—mythic, larger than life, humbling.

And then there is the fact that Walter almost never threw a curve. In other words, everybody knew what he was up to out there but still couldn't hit him. There is the size of that right arm: pictures show it reaching halfway down his thigh. Like Einstein's brain and Caruso's lungs, Walter's right arm was different from yours and mine. With it he fired that little ball with an almost underhand buggy-whip snap which apparently placed a minimum of strain on it.

And then, of course, there is his record. Walter had batters fanning the air in such numbers that his totals still dominate in an age when batters strike out at least a third more often than they used to. His lifetime strikeout total of 3,508 remains the mountaintop figure. He led in strikeouts 12 times, with a high of 313 in 1910. He pitched 21 years (1907–1927) for a Washington club that was generally out of contention, and he still won 416 games, more than any pitcher in this century. In 1913 he was 36–7 (one of 2 30-game seasons; he won 32 the year before), with a 1.09 earned-run average and 12 shutouts. Lifetime, he hurled a record 113 shutouts. His career ERA for close to 6,000 innings is 2.17. His ERA started with a magical "1" 11 times, and 12 times he won 20 or better, including a string of 7 straight seasons (1910–1916) of 25 wins or better, a staggering statistic.

They called him "The Big Train," which dates him. He was one of the most beloved of all ballplayers, by all accounts a kindly man (which is just as well; an evil-tempered Walter Johnson is frightening to contemplate). He was known to let up on young players in lopsided games to give them a chance.

His control was superb, for which American League batters of his time gave prayerful thanks. Walter was in fact so conscious of his terrific speed that he was reluctant to pitch in close, thus giving the batters a slight edge. It didn't help them very much.

Walter Johnson in 1913, when he won 36 games . . .

. . . and had an earned-run average of 1.09.

Tobacco-chewing George Brett

George Brett

Only 28 years old as he went into the 1981 season, Kansas City Royals third baseman George Brett seems well on his way toward becoming one of the great all-time names at the position.

A polished fielder, George is even more renowned for his bat, one of the wickedest in baseball. Although the left-handed-swinging Brett has hit more than 20 home runs three times since becoming a regular in 1974, he is primarily a line-drive hitter, sending ringing shots in all directions.

In 1976 Brett derailed Rod Carew's bid for a fifth straight batting title with a .333 average, a title he won on the last day of the season, edging out Carew and teammate Hal McRae. In 1980 he flirted with .400 for most of the season and finally wound up batting a remarkable .390.

Along with his batting titles, Brett has already tied a major-league record for leading in triples in 2 consecutive years, 1975 and 1976, with 13 and 14 3-baggers, then leading for a third time in 1979 with 20, the most in the American League in 30 years. He also led in doubles in 1978 with 45. In addition, he has led the league 3 times in hits, with 195 in 1975, 215 in 1976, and 212 in 1979. In 1976 he was first in total bases, with 298.

In 1976 he established a major-league record by getting 3 or more hits for 6 consecutive games.

Going into the 1981 season with a .319 average for his 7 full years, George Brett's greatness is predicated on achievement and even more so on promise of things to come.

Robin Roberts

Robin Roberts pitched his greatest game on the last day of the 1950 season, against the Brooklyn Dodgers. With the pennant riding on every pitch, Roberts, making his third start in 5 days during the stretch run, outdueled Don Newcombe in a 10-inning 4-1 victory that put the Phillies in the World Series.

That game typified the enormously talented Philadelphia right-hander's performance—he was tireless and he responded to pressure with his finest effort. Pitching from 1948 through 1966, the smooth-working Roberts won 286 games. The only National League pitchers with more wins in this century are Christy Mathewson and Grover Cleveland Alexander.

Roberts, who threw a low, rising fastball with superb control, put in his best years from 1950 to 1955, when he won 20 or better in all 6 seasons, with a peak year of 28-7 in 1952. He led in games won from 1952 to 1955; he also led twice in strikeouts, 5 times in innings pitched, and 5 times in complete games. The only National League right-handers to top his 305 complete games in the modern era are Christy Mathewson, Grover Cleveland Alexander, and Burleigh Grimes.

He could get a needed strikeout in the ninth inning by suddenly firing harder than he had in the first. When a teammate once asked him what enabled him to do this, Roberts replied casually, "Oh, you can't see that. It comes from inside." Unwittingly, the unaffected Roberts had yielded the secret of greatness when under pressure: it comes from inside.

New York Giants' left-hander Johnny Antonelli **(left)** *and Robin Roberts in 1956*

Chief Bender in 1904

"Chief" Bender

Connie Mack managed, among others, Rube Waddell, Eddie Plank, Jack Coombs, and Lefty Grove. However, the greatest money pitcher he ever had, Mack said, was Chief Bender.

Charles Albert Bender, called "Chief" because of his Chippewa heritage, was a classy right-hander who worked for the Philadelphia Athletics from 1903 to 1914, then pitched in the Federal League in 1915, and finished up his career with the Phillies for 2 seasons. His lifetime record is 208–112, good for a .650 winning percentage.

Bothered by various illnesses during his career, Bender did not log the innings pitched nor the win totals of some of his contemporaries. His best season was 1910, when he was 23–5, completing 25 out of 28 starts and posting a 1.58 earned-run average. The Chief's .821 winning percentage led the league that year, and he led again the next year with .773 on the strength of a 17–5 record. He led a third time in 1914, his 17–3 record giving him an .850 win percentage. Only Lefty Grove has topped the league more times in winning percentage (5).

Bender was a highly intelligent man, proud of his Indian background. He took a wry view of the fans who twitted him with war cries when he appeared on the field. The Chief's way of responding was to turn to them, cup his hands around his mouth and shout back, "Foreigners! Foreigners!"

Frankie Frisch in 1923

Frankie Frisch

How good was Frankie Frisch? His record, while outstanding (lifetime batting average .316 for 19 years), does not really have a neon quality on the printed page. Between 1919, when he came straight from the campus of Fordham University to John McGraw's infield, and 1937, when he retired as an active player with the Cardinals, Frisch put in 17 full seasons and batted over .300 in 13 of them, 3 times batting in the .340s. He collected more than 200 hits 3 times, with a league-leading 223 in 1923, and 3 times led the league in stolen bases. From 1925 to the end of his career he never struck out more than 17 times in a season, while coming to bat well over 500 times each year. His total strikeouts for over 9,000 at bats is only 272.

The record is good, but Frisch is remembered by his contemporaries primarily for his intangibles. He was a dynamic player, a ferocious competitor. If he cost a run with an error, teammate Bill Hallahan remembers, he would come back into the dugout snarling and red-faced. "He would get that run back for you by sheer grit," Hallahan recalled. "He

would get on base somehow—a walk, a bunt, somehow—steal second, maybe third, and come around. That's the way he played ball."

How good was he? Well, good enough to be traded for Rogers Hornsby. Hornsby was the idol of St. Louis and the trade caused an uproar among Cardinal's fans. But after watching Frisch's relentless play for a year,

Rival player-managers before the start of the 1934 World Series: Mickey Cochrane (left) and Frankie Frisch

Frankie Frisch defending a rather battered third base

Cardinal's fans were willing to forgive and forget, and were in fact delighted with the Fordham Flash.

Frisch drove the Cardinals to pennants in 1928, 1930, 1931, and as player-manager of the Gashouse Gang in 1934. All told, he played in 8 World Series, including 4 with the Giants from 1921 to 1924.

McGraw did not want to trade his sizzling second baseman, but after years of McGraw's taunts and hide-ripping criticism, the fiery Frisch rebelled. He would not take it. The verbal battles between McGraw and Frisch steamed the air in the Giant clubhouse until finally, one day in 1926, the raging Frisch jumped the team and went home. He returned soon enough, but the enmity between player and manager was by this time too strong for reconciliation and the famous trade was made.

Frisch was a switch hitter, equally strong from either side of the plate. Possessed of great speed afoot, he was also one of the finest fielding second basemen in National League history. He led in fielding percentage 4 times, and his 641 assists in 1927 remains the record for National League second basemen.

In 1934 Frisch led the raucous Gashouse Gang into the World Series against the Detroit Tigers. In the decisive seventh game, the 36-year-old veteran had what was probably his greatest moment on a ball field. In the top of the third inning the score was 0–0, there was 1 out, and the Cardinals had men on second and third. Tiger manager Mickey Cochrane decided to walk the next batter, Jack Rothrock, in order to set up a double-play situation with Frisch at bat. It was a mistake. A player like Frisch was a zealous enough competitor without receiving so naked a challenge. Detroit right-hander Eldon Auker got 2 strikes on Frank, but Frisch hung tough, fouling off 4 pitches before clearing the bases with a line double to right field. That opened the floodgates to a 7-run inning and an eventual 11–0 victory and the World Championship.

It was just a few years earlier that a reporter had approached Joe McCarthy, then managing the Cubs, and asked him to create a composite that would embody the perfect player. The reporter suggested this one's arm, that one's speed, another's hitting, another's defense. Finally McCarthy interrupted the man and said, "Why don't you just say Frank Frisch and be done with it?"

Frisch is out at home.

Herb Pennock in 1926

Herb Pennock

Herb Pennock came to the big leagues with the Philadelphia Athletics in 1912 at the age of 18. Two years later the young gentleman—and he was, all his life, a most elegant gentleman—was 11–4 and helped the A's into the World Series. A year later Connie Mack broke up his team and sent Herb to the Red Sox. There Pennock pitched well for losing teams until 1923, when he was traded to the Yankees, part of the disgraceful 1-way shuttle of star players between Boston and New York in those years.

With the Yankees, Pennock hit his stride. He was 19–6 in 1923, 21–9 the next year, 23–11 in 1926, 19–8 in 1927, and 17–6 the next year. His manager, Miller Huggins, considered the stylish Pennock—"stylish" is the word most frequently associated with Pennock's mound performances—the greatest left-hander of all time. Probably this was managerial pride speaking, but Pennock was one of the best. He was a control pitcher, and what he controlled was a tantalizing assortment of breaking pitches. "He didn't throw it past you," Lloyd Waner, who faced him in the 1927 Series, recalled. "He just made you hit it at somebody."

Pennock, who won 241 games and lost 162 in his 22-year big-league career, was at his best in World Series competition. His post-season record was spotless: 5–0, with an earned-run average of 1.95 for 55 innings of work.

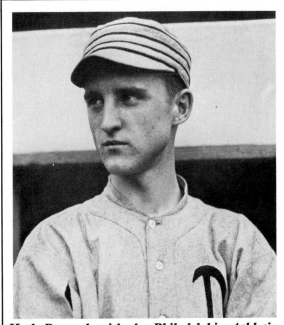

Herb Pennock with the Philadelphia Athletics in 1914

Eddie Plank in 1911

Eddie Plank

Smoky Joe Wood was looking back nearly 70 years when he recalled Eddie Plank, the Philadelphia Athletics' great left-hander from 1901 to 1914. "He was very studious out there," Smoky Joe said. "He used to pitch to spots. They didn't do that much in those days. But Eddie Plank did it." One must assume that Plank hit his spot more often than not, since he became the first pitcher in the modern era to win 300 games, compiling a 305–181 career record.

Since he didn't reach the big leagues until he was 25, Plank had to win often and win big in order to reach 300, and this is exactly what he did. He won 17 in his first season, then went over 20 in 5 of his next 6 seasons, winning 26 and 25 in 1904 and 1905, another 24 in 1907, 22 in 1911, and 26 again in 1912.

The quiet, poker-faced Plank was born in Gettysburg and went to college there. During his college days he occasionally hooked up in pitching duels with a Bucknell student named Christy Mathewson. The two would later oppose each other in several World Series.

Plank shares with Mickey Lolich the American League record for consecutive years of 100 or more strikeouts by a left-hander, 13. His 64 lifetime shutouts rank him fourth behind Walter Johnson, Grover Cleveland Alexander, and Christy Mathewson among pitchers since 1900.

Disdaining the spitball, shine ball, emery ball, and other trick pitches of the day, Plank relied on his fastball and curve, studiously thrown to his spots.

Joe Sewell in 1923

Joe Sewell

Joe Sewell remains the most uncanny hitter in baseball history. Of all the men who have ever stood at home plate, he was the most difficult to strike out. Between 1925 and 1929 he never played in fewer than 152 games a season, never had fewer than 569 at bats, and his strikeout totals read 4, 6, 7, 9, and 4. In 1931 he came to bat 484 times and struck out 8 times, then in 1932 outdid himself with 3 whiffs in 503 at bats. The next year, his last in the big leagues, Joe fanned 4 times in 524 visits to the plate. Overall, for 7,132 at bats in a career that ran from 1920 to 1932, Joe struck out just 114 times—a single year's work for many big-league hitters today.

He was no banjo hitter either, hitting more than 40 doubles 5 times, leading the league with 45 in 1924. He batted in over 90 runs in a season 5 times. As befits a man who always laid his bat on the ball, his lifetime batting average is .312, with season highs of .353 and .336.

No man ever came to the big leagues under more unhappy circumstances. Joe was the shortstop who Cleveland brought up in August 1920 to replace Ray Chapman, who had died from the effects of being hit in the head by a Carl Mays fastball. The 21-year-old rookie played well down the stretch, his .329 batting average helping the Indians to a pennant.

And what was his great secret at home plate? He imparted it to an interviewer many years later. "You've got to keep your eye on the ball," said Mr. Sewell.

Burleigh Grimes

Burleigh Grimes will always be remembered as one of the greatest of the spitball pitchers, though Grimes himself insisted that his fastball was generally his number 1 pitch. The old spitballer also threw a curve, slider, change of pace, and screwball, and threw them with cold, belligerent efficiency. He was a brutally fierce, unsmiling competitor for the 19 years he pitched in the big leagues.

Grimes came to the majors in 1916 with Pittsburgh. In 1917 he was 3–16 and the Pirates were glad to trade him to Brooklyn. The famous borough agreed with Grimes, who turned his record around to 19–9 and was off to a career as one of Brooklyn's greatest pitchers. "Boily," as his name sounded on the lips of Dodger fans, pitched for Brooklyn for 9 years, winning more than 20 4 times. Thereafter he began his travels, pitching for 8 teams over the next 8 years. Back with Pittsburgh in 1928, he put in his best season, with 25 wins.

Overall, Grimes won 270 and lost 212. He pitched 314 complete games, a figure topped only by those two classics, Christy Mathewson and Grover Cleveland Alexander, among National League righties in this century. He led the league in complete games 4 times and in victories twice.

Burleigh was the pitching hero of the 1931 World Series. Working for the Cardinals, he stopped the powerful Philadelphia Athletics' bid for a third straight World Championship, winning 2 games, including the decisive seventh game.

Arky Vaughan in 1942

"Arky" Vaughan

Along with Johnny Mize, Arky Vaughan is the Hall of Fame's most conspicuous and inexplicable oversight. Sometimes it seems that members of the Committee on Veterans never consult a record book. If they did, they would see that Joseph Floyd "Arky" Vaughan arrived in Pittsburgh in 1932 as the Pirates' regular shortstop and began hitting .300 with machine-gun regularity. For his first 10 years Vaughan hit above that yardstick figure, climbing to a titanic, league-leading .385 in 1935. No National Leaguer has topped it since.

Vaughan's lifetime .318 batting average is higher than that of any Hall of Fame shortstop with the exception of Honus Wagner.

Arky was a do-it-all ballplayer. He possessed exceptionally fine running speed and was a strong fielder, leading National League shortstops 3 times in putouts and 3 times in assists. Eagle-eyed at the bat, he seldom struck out (only 276 times in 6,622 at bat) and is coholder of the league record for leading in bases on balls for 3 consecutive years (1934–1936). He also led in runs scored 3 times and in triples 3 times.

Vaughan, who finished his career with the Dodgers in 1948, was a quiet, modest, self-effacing man. His premature death by drowning in 1952 took him from the scene at the age of 40.

Baseball owes this fine athlete and gentleman some long overdue recognition.

Rod Carew in 1968

Rod Carew

When baseball people are asked to explain the general decline in batting averages from what they were in past years, the explanations are various: night ball, the slider, relief-pitching specialists, swinging from the end of the bat. If all these reasons make sense, and they do, how then do we explain the phenomenon called Rod Carew?

Carew, who joined the Minnesota Twins as a 21-year-old second baseman in 1967, has posted the most consistently high batting averages since the heyday of Ted Williams and Stan Musial. In 1969 he hit .332, in an injury-shortened 1970 he hit .366, and beginning in 1973 through 1980 his batting averages read .350, .364, .359, .331, .388, .333, .318, and .331. Carew has won batting titles in 1969, 1972, 1973, 1974, 1975, 1977, and 1978. That adds up to 7, tying him with Rogers Hornsby and Stan Musial. Only Honus Wagner (8) and Ty Cobb (12) have more. Carew is one of the greatest hitters in big-league history.

Rod has led the league 3 times in hits, with a high of 239 in 1977, and twice in triples. A speedster on the bases, he has stolen more than 30 bases in a season 4 times, including stealing home 16 times in his career. Since 1920 only Frankie Frisch and Jackie Robinson, both with 19, have done better. In 1969

he tied Pete Reiser's major-league single-season record with 7 steals of home.

Going into the 1981 season, Carew, who joined the California Angels as a free agent in 1979, has a career batting average of .333.

Dizzy Dean with the Cardinals in 1932, with third baseman Pepper Martin in the background

"Dizzy" Dean

According to Jay Hanna "Dizzy" Dean, if you said you were going to pitch a shutout and then went ahead and did it, it wasn't bragging. There are no statistics on shutouts predicted, but if there were, Dean would no doubt own that record.

He was an exuberant, garrulous, witty, lovable man whose self-confidence was unimpeachable. Pitching for the St. Louis Cardinals in the early 1930s, he caught the imagination of a Depression-bleak nation and generated much of what little joy and excitement existed in those lean years.

The son of an Arkansas sharecropper, Dean came to the Cardinals in 1932 and promptly posted an 18–15 record, leading the league in innings pitched, strikeouts, and shutouts. A year later he was 20–18 and again the strikeout leader. In 1934 he broke through to greatness with a 30–7 record, the National League's first 30-game winner since Grover Cleveland Alexander in 1917. He led that year in wins, winning percentage, complete games, strikeouts, and shutouts. Then, with his brother Paul (whom many said threw

Dizzy Dean in 1929

harder than Dizzy), he went on to defeat the Tigers in the World Series (each of the Deans won 2 games), including a seventh game 11–0 shutout.

In 1935 he won 28 and lost 12, completing 29 of 36 starts, and took his fourth consecutive strikeout title. In 1936 he was 24–13, starting and relieving, completing 28 of 34 starts. He was 25 years old, the greatest

The Dean brothers: Paul (left) and Dizzy

drawing card in baseball, and, everyone felt, his biggest years lay ahead.

He started off well again in 1937 and was selected to start the All-Star game for the National League. Pitching to the American League's Earl Averill in the third inning, Dean was hit on the foot by a screeching line drive and suffered a broken toe. He should have rested for several weeks until the toe mended. But the restless Dean was eager to return to work, and his eagerness was not discouraged by the Cardinal management, who were not happy having their top drawing card out of action.

Favoring his injured toe as he pitched, Dean effected an unnatural motion and in so doing hurt his arm severely and permanently. Almost overnight the blazing fastball was gone, never to return. He ended the 1937 season with a 13–10 record.

The Cardinals sold their dead-armed pitcher to the Cubs the next year. Pitching on guile, guts, and memory, Dean was 7–1, helping the Cubs to a pennant. In the 1938 Series he baffled the powerhouse Yankees with slow curves for 7 innings, but then the Bombers caught up with him. It was Dean's last flirtation with greatness on a baseball diamond. In and out for the next 3 years, he won a total of 9 games. He retired at the age of 30 with a 150–83 won-lost record and a .644 winning percentage.

Dizzy Dean remains one of the very few ballplayers whose name has slipped into American folklore; it is still recognizable today to many people, both in and out of baseball.

Alphabetical Listing

Hank Aaron   147
Grover Cleveland Alexander   21
Luis Aparicio   107
Luke Appling   53
"Home Run" Baker   137
Ernie Banks   125
Johnny Bench   173
"Chief" Bender   251
"Yogi" Berra   29
George Brett   247
Lou Brock   101
"Three-Fingered" Brown   77
Roy Campanella   7
Rod Carew   267
Steve Carlton   195
Hal Chase   129
Roberto Clemente   11
Ty Cobb   97
"Mickey" Cochrane   157
Eddie Collins   5
Jimmy Collins   65
Sam Crawford   43
"Kiki" Cuyler   19
"Dizzy" Dean   269
Bill Dickey   27
Joe DiMaggio   187
Bob Feller   31
Wes Ferrell   237
"Whitey" Ford   123
George Foster   47
Jimmie Foxx   39
Frankie Frisch   253
Steve Garvey   217
Lou Gehrig   81

Charlie Gehringer   113
Bob Gibson   25
"Goose" Goslin   93
Hank Greenberg   87
Burleigh Grimes   263
"Lefty" Grove   49
"Chick" Hafey   55
"Gabby" Hartnett   221
Harry Heilmann   241
Rogers Hornsby   165
Carl Hubbell   69
"Shoeless" Joe Jackson   203
Walter Johnson   243
Addie Joss   151
Sandy Koufax   119
Napoleon Lajoie   185
Ernie Lombardi   37
Fred Lynn   135
Ted Lyons   235
Mickey Mantle   223
Juan Marichal   183
Christy Mathewson   71
Willie Mays   59
"Iron Man" McGinnity   163
Joe Medwick   181
Johnny Mize   239
Joe Morgan   115
Stan Musial   127
Tony Oliva   45
Mel Ott   117
Jim Palmer   15
Dave Parker   159
Herb Pennock   257
Eddie Plank   259

Pete Reiser   153
Jim Rice   201
Robin Roberts   249
Brooks Robinson   197
Frank Robinson   207
Jackie Robinson   89
Pete Rose   1
Edd Roush   211
"Babe" Ruth   139
Mike Schmidt   35
Herb Score   95
Tom Seaver   75
Joe Sewell   261
Al Simmons   67
George Sisler   79
"Duke" Snider   17
Warren Spahn   133
Tris Speaker   209
Bill Terry   9
"Pie" Traynor   105
"Dazzy" Vance   169
"Arky" Vaughan   265
"Rube" Waddell   109
Honus Wagner   213
Ed Walsh   149
Paul Waner   231
"Zack" Wheat   219
Ted Williams   175
"Smoky" Joe Wood   57
Carl Yastrzemski   229
"Cy" Young   227
Ross Youngs   171

About the Authors

LAWRENCE RITTER is the author of *The Glory of Their Times,* a book which the *New York Times* praised as "the best sports book in recent memory," and coauthor of *The Image of Their Greatness: An Illustrated History of Baseball from 1900 to the Present.* When he is not thinking about, writing about, or watching a baseball game, he is serving as a professor of economics and finance at New York University. Mr. Ritter lives in Manhattan.

DONALD HONIG is considered to be one of the greatest walking encyclopedias on baseball. He has written five other books on the subject, including *Baseball When the Grass Was Real* and *The Image of Their Greatness* (with Lawrence Ritter). In addition, he is the author of eleven novels and a number of books for children. A native New Yorker, Mr. Honig now lives in Cromwell, Connecticut.